The book consists of an image part and a text part, which are connected by a linking system that looks like this.

1. IMAGE LINKS

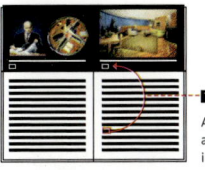

171 Appears in the text and links to one page in the image book.

2. LINKS TO IMAGES COVERING THE TWO BOOKS

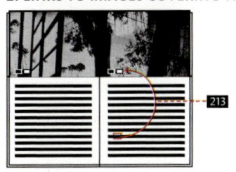

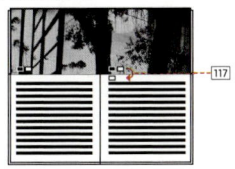

2.1 Image link also appears in the text and points to one page in the image book.

2.2 There, next to the page number, is the corresponding page in the text book.

2.3 Return to text using **3. LINKS TO TEXT PASSAGES**

3. LINKS TO TEXT PASSAGES

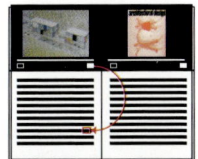

Indicate where the reference to the image appears in the text.

INDEX

Introduction: Built in the USA
4, 5, 6, 7, 8, 9, 10, 11, 12, 13, 14, 15, 16, 17, 18, 19, 20, 21, 22, 23

Chapter 1: 1949
24, 25, 26, 27, 28, 29, 30, 31, 32, 33, 34, 35, 36, 37, 38, 39, 40, 41, 42, 43, 44, 45, 46, 47, 48, 49, 50, 51, 52, 53, 54, 55, 55, 56, 57, 58, 59, 60, 61, 62, 63, 64, 65, 66, 67, 68, 69, 70, 71, 72, 73, 74, 75, 76, 77, 78, 79, 80, 81, 82, 83, 84, 85, 86, 87, 88, 89, 90, 91, 92, 93, 94, 95, 96, 97, 98, 99

Chapter 2: DDU at MoMA
100, 101, 102, 103, 104, 105, 106, 107, 108, 109, 110, 111, 112, 113, 114, 115, 116, 117, 118, 119, 120, 121

Chapter 3: The Eames House
122, 123, 124, 125, 126, 127, 128, 129, 130, 131, 132, 133, 134, 135, 136, 137, 138, 139, 140, 141, 142, 143, 144, 145, 146, 147, 148, 149, 150, 151, 152, 153, 154, 155, 156, 157, 158, 159, 160, 161, 162, 163, 164, 165, 166, 167, 168, 169, 170, 171, 172, 173, 174, 175, 176, 177, 178, 179, 180, 181, 182, 183, 184, 185, 186, 187

Chapter 4: The Lawn at War
188, 189, 190, 191, 192, 193, 194, 195, 196, 197, 198, 199, 200, 201, 202, 203, 204, 205, 206, 207, 208, 209, 210, 211

Chapter 5: **X-Ray Architecture**

212 213 214 215 216 217 218 219 220 221 223 224 225 226 227 228 229 230 231 232 233 234 235 236 237 238 239 240 241 242 243 244 245 246 247 248 249 250 251 252 253 254 255 256 257 258 259 260 261 262 263 264 265 266 267 268 269 270 271 272 273 274 275 276 277 278 279 280 281 282 283 284 285 286 287 288 289 290 291

Chapter 6: **Unbreathed Air**

292 293 294 295 296 297 298 299 300 301 302 303 304 305 306 307 308 309 310 311 312 313 314 315 316 317 318 319 320 321 322 323 324 325 326 327 328 329 330 331 332 333 334 335 336 337 338 339 340 341 342 343 344 345 346 347 348 349

Chapter 7: **Enclosed by Images**

350 351 352 353 354 355 356 357 358 359 360 361 362 363 364 365 366 367 368 369 370 371 372 373 374 375 376 377 378 379 380 381 382 383 384 385 386 387 388 389 390 391 392 393 394 395 396 397 398 399 400 401 402 403 404 405 406 407 408 409

Chapter 8: **The Underground House**

410 411 412 413 414 415 416 417 418 419 420 421 422 423 424 425 426 427 428 429 430 431 432 433 434 435 436 437 438 439 440 441 442 443 444 445 446 447

Beatriz Colomina (Curriculum vitae and foto)

448

Cover of catalog to the exhibition Modern Architecture at the Museum of Modern Art,

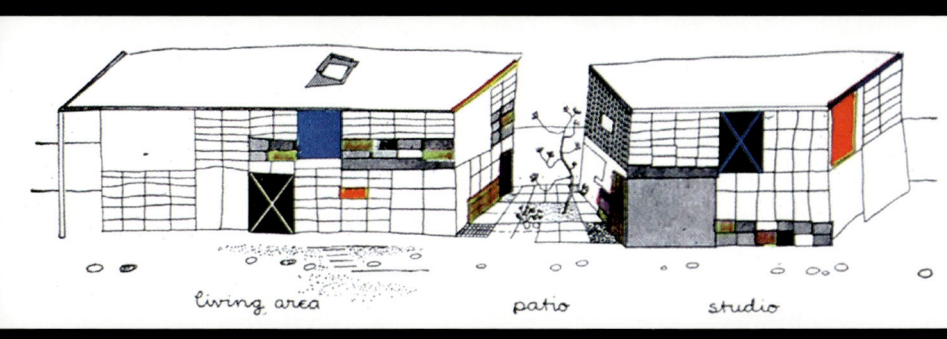

Charles and Ray Eames's Diagram of the Eames House.
From "Life in a Chinese Kite," *Architectural Forum*, September 1950.

☒☐ Eduardo Paolozzi, *Dr. Pepper*, dated 1948.
Collage on paper. 14 1/4 x 9 3/8 in. Collection of the artist.
☐☒ Eduardo Paolozzi, *Psychological Atlas and four other scrapbooks*, 1947–53.
Collage. 9 1/8 x 6 5/8 in. By courtesy of the artist and the Trustees of the
Victoria and Albert Museum, London.

"Los Angeles: The Art of Living Bumper to Bumper."
From *Look* magazine.

"Los Angeles: The Art of Living Bumper to Bumper."
From *Look* magazine.

"Los Angeles: The Art of Living Bumper to Bumper." From *Look* magazine.

10 Ray Eames color plan of the Eames Office room display.

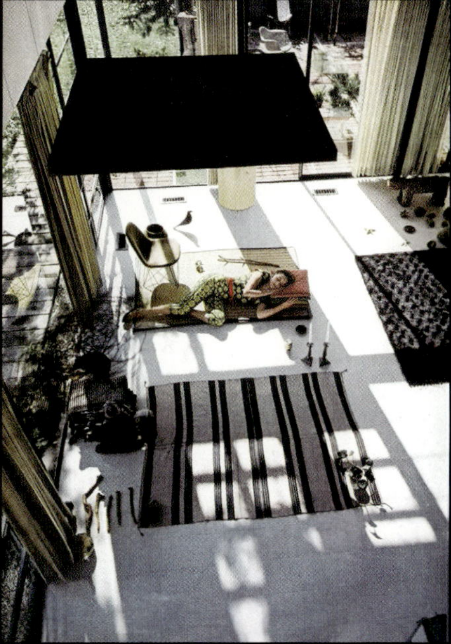

☒☐ Fashion shoot in the Eames House.
From *Vogue*, April 15, 1954.
☐☒ "California's Bold Look," page from a fashion-magazine feature shot in the Eames House.
From *Life*, June 1954.

CASE STUDY HOUSES

8 AND 9

BY CHARLES EAMES AND EERO SAARINEN, ARCHITECTS

This is ground in meadow and hill, protected on all sides from intrusive developments free of the usual surrounding clutter, safe from urban clatter; not, however, removed from the necessary conveniences and the reassurances of city living.

Two houses for people of different occupations but parallel interests. Both, however, determinedly agreed on the necessity of privacy, on the right to choose privacy from one another and anyone else.

While these houses are not to be considered as solutions of typical living problems; through meeting specific and rather special needs, some contribution to the need of the typical might be developed. The whole solution proceeds from an attempt to say space in direct relation to the personal and professional needs of the individuals revolving around and within the living units inasmuch as the greater part of work or preparation for work will originate here. These houses must function as an integral part of the living pattern of the occupants and will therefore be completely "used" in a very full and real sense. "Houses" in these cases means center of productive activities.

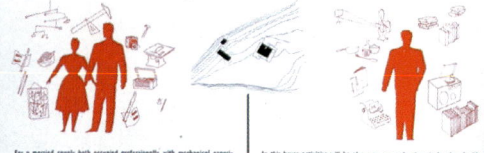

For a married couple both occupied professionally with mechanical experiment and graphic presentation. Work and recreation are involved in general activities. Day and night, work and play, concentration, relaxation with friend and foe, all intermingled personally and professionally with mutual interest. Basically apartment dwellers, there is a conscious effort made to be free of complications relating to maintenance. The house must make an instinct demands for itself, but rather aid as background for life in work. This house—in its free relation the ground, the trees, the sea—with constant proximity to the whole vast order of nature acts as re-orientor and "shock absorber" and should provide the needed relaxations from the daily complications arising within problems.

In this house activities will be of a more general nature to be shared with more people and more things. It will also be used as a returning place for relaxation and refilling, a place to be alone for preparation of work, and with matters and concerns of personal choosing. A place for the kind of relaxed privacy necessary for the development and preparation of ideas to be continued in professional work centers. The occupant will need space used elastically where many or few people can be accommodated within the areas appropriate to each needs. Intimate conversation, groups in discussion, the use of a projection machine for amusement and education, and facilities for self-indulgent hobbies, i.e., cooking and the entertainment of very close friends.

13　Charles Eames and John Entenza.

14 | Marcel Breuer, House in the Museum Garden, MoMA, New York, 1949

Literally mountains of material have been created by industry under the pressures of war conditions. Not only American industry but also world industry has fully demonstrated its ability to create an abundance of goods for man's needs. But more important than this important fact is man's growing awareness of his real power through the machine. His absolute knowledge of not only an industrial potential but also the accomplished fact of an industrial reality so vast, so overpowering that it becomes the one great common denominator of the life of all mankind.

True mass production has won the respect of all people because it has been able to put into their hands the weapons by which their lives have been saved in war. Man now knows that mass production properly directed and properly disciplined will not only save lives but also set them free. The one outstanding fact of our time is that this c a n be done. We no longer lack the means. It is now only a matter of directing our wills and our intelligence to the proper use of the mountains of materials and technologies at our disposal in order to solve the most pressing problems which concern the material welfare of mankind.

Science in industry cannot be expected to function if it must make compromises in terms of political minorities, committments-to-the-past or prejudices concerning the future.

Walter and Ise Gropius at breakfast in their house in Lincoln, Massachusetts.

Le Corbusier with Walter and Alma Gropius at the Café des Deux Magots in Paris.

20 Ray Eames's desk, 1976.

Details of Eames House and studio.
Photos: Charles Eames.

Pierre Koenig, Case Study House #21, Los Angeles, 1958. Living room. Photo: Julius Shulman.

☒ ☐ Cover of Le Corbusier, *Vers une architecture*, 1923.
☐ ☒ Cover of *G*, no. 3, June 1924, with the elevation of Mies van der Rohe's Glass Skyscraper of 1922.

L'ESPRIT NOUVEAU

REVUE INTERNATIONALE D'ESTHÉTIQUE

DIRECTEUR : PAUL DERMÉE

ESTHÉTIQUE EXPÉRIMENTALE
SCIENCES PHILOSOPHIE ARCHITECTURE
LITTÉRATURE MUSIQUE
ESTHÉTIQUE DE L'INGÉNIEUR
LE THÉÂTRE LE MUSIC-HALL LE CINÉMA LE CIRQUE LES SPORTS
LE COSTUME LE LIVRE LE MEUBLE
ESTHÉTIQUE DE LA VIE MODERNE

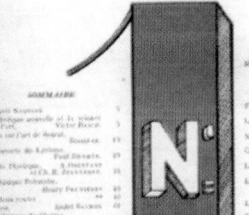

SOMMAIRE

L'Esprit Nouveau	3
L'archéologie nouvelle et la science de l'art.... Victor Basch	7
Notes sur l'art actuel	
Ozenfant-Jeanneret	15
Découverte du Lyrisme... Paul Dermée	17
Sur la Physique... V. Posener et Ch. E. Jeanneret	
La Musique Polytonale... Henry Prunières	
Les deux risques... Albert Gleizes	
Picasso... André Salmon	
L'Esthétique du Cheval... R. Francé	

DANS CE NUMÉRO

30 photogravures et deux reproductions aux trois couleurs.

Paul Lapparent	
L'Opéra, art antimusical... Alain Savinio	
Notes sur les années 1915-1916, et de La-vie-des-lettres	
Calligrammes et Architecture Louis Aragon	
Les Expositions (Pictet) G. Ribemont-Dessaignes	
Les Directives de langue espagnole d'aujourd'hui	
La nouvelle poésie allemande Yvan Goll	
Échos de l'Hôtel Drouot	

PRIX NET : 6 francs (France)
POUR TOUS PAYS

ÉDITIONS DE L'ESPRIT NOUVEAU
SOCIÉTÉ ANONYME AU CAPITAL DE 100.000 FRANCS
75, QUAI DE CONTI
PARIS (VI°)

26 | Le Corbusier and Amédée Ozenfant in the Eiffel Tower, 1923

27 Exhibition Modern Architecture at MoMA, New York, 1932.

28 Philip Johnson, Glass House, New Canaan, Connecticut, 1949.

Mies van der Rohe, Farnsworth House, Plano, Illinois, 1945–50.
Photo: Hedrich-Blessing, Chicago.

Charles and Ray Eames, Eames House, Pacific Palisades, 1949.

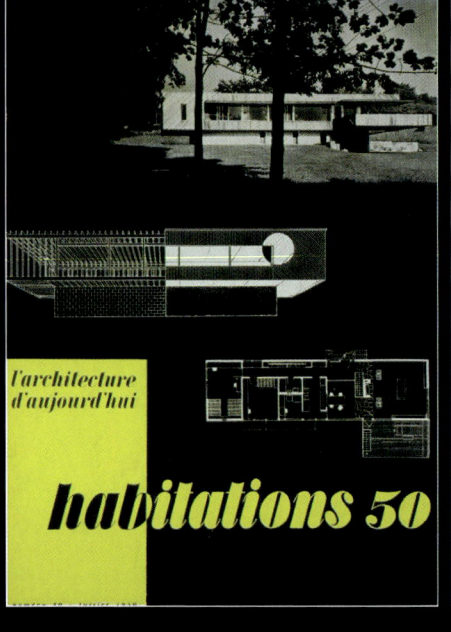

france	2	henri et jean prouvé.
	6	guy lagneau, jovan dimitriejvic, marcel gascoin.
	8	pierre pinsard.
	10	c. mazet.
angleterre	12	ernö goldfinger et gerald flower.
belgique	14	claude laurens.
	18	jacques dupuis.
espagne	19	j. a. coderch de sen:menat et valls verges.
cuba	22	junco, gaston et dominguez.
italie	24	franco buzzi et pietro porcinai.
suisse	26	carlo et rino tami.
états-unis	28	richard j. neutra.
	36	marcel breuer.
	48	philip c. johnson.
	51	pierre chareau.
	52	paul laszlo.
	55	paul rudolph et ralph s. twitchell.
	67	gordon drake.
	70	ralph rapson et john van der meulen.
brésil	73	oscar niemeyer soares.

L'architecture d'aujourd'hui, July 1950. Cover and table of contents.

33 Pierre Chareau, Robert Motherwell Studio-House in East Hampton, New York, 1948.

Paul Rudolph and Ralph Twitchell, Healy Guest House (Cocoon House), Siesta Key, Florida, 1950.

35 Healy Guest House. Interior view.

36 Charles and Ray Eames, Eames House, 1949. Living room view with Christmas decorations.

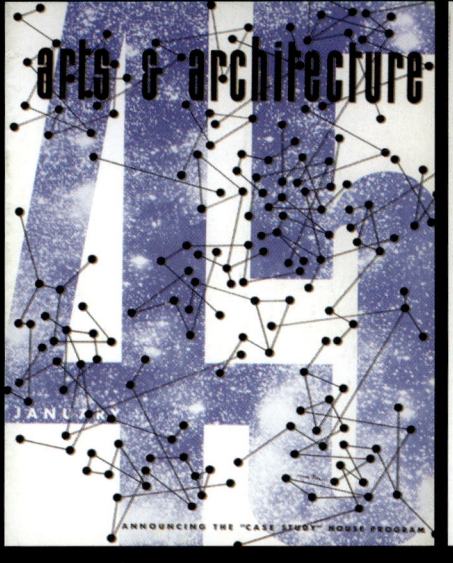

⊠☐ Cover of *Arts & Architecture*, January 1945, announcing the Case Study House Program.
   Cover design: Herbert Matter.
☐⊠ Announcement of the Case Study House Program.
   From *Arts & Architecture*, January 1945.

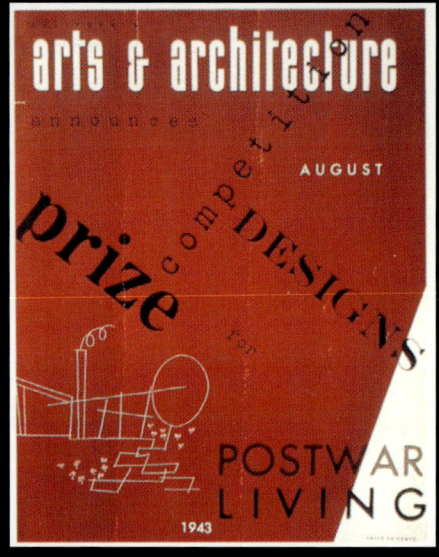 

☒☐ Cover of *Arts & Architecture*, August 1943, announcing the competition Designs for Postwar Living. Cover design: Ray Eames.

☐☒ Plywood for War, Later for Peace advertisement for George E. Ram Company Vital Victory Materials. From: *Arts & Architecture*, August 1943.

LES MAISONS "VOISIN"

Il semblait jusqu'ici qu'une maison fut lourdement attachée au sol par la profondeur de ses fondations et la pesanteur de ses murs épais ; cette maison, c'était le symbole de l'immuabilité, la « maison natale », le « berceau de famille », etc. Ce n'est point par un artifice que la maison Voisin est l'une des premières à marquer le contre-pied même de cette conception. La science de bâtir a évolué d'une manière foudroyante en ces derniers temps ; l'art de bâtir a pris racine fortement dans la science.

L'énoncé du problème a fourni à lui seul les moyens de réalisation et, incontinent, s'affirme ici fortement l'immense révolution dans laquelle est entrée l'architecture : lorsqu'on modifie à tel point le mode de bâtir, automatiquement l'esthétique de la construction se trouve bouleversée. Cet énoncé est le suivant ; il fut formulé par des soldats en pleine guerre qui se dirent en voyant tomber tant d'hommes autour d'eux :

Plywood leg splints designed by Charles and Ray Eames, 1943.

Mass production of plywood leg splints.

43 Frank Brothers advertisement for plywood cabinets designed by Charles and Ray Eames, 1950.

44 | Charles Eames sitting in the plywood lounge chair, 1946

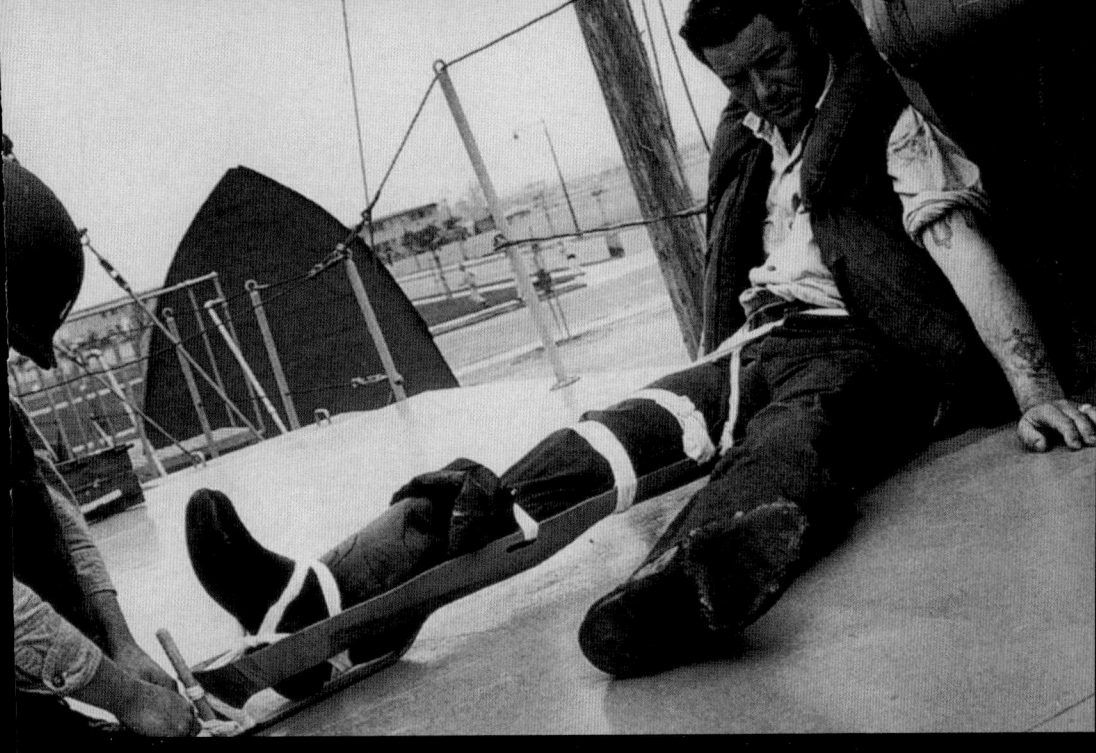

45 Demonstration of the splint in use during the war, 1943.

46 Herbert Matter's son, Alexander (Pundy), sitting on an Eames molded plywood elephant.

47　Charles and Ray Eames at Christmas 1944, with plywood sculpture by Ray.

Charles Eames and Eero Saarinen, Case Study House #9, under construction, 1945.

49 Charles and Ray Eames, Case Study House #8, under construction.

Charles and Ray Eames with their first Case Study House model, which they called "Bridge House," 1945.

51 Mies van der Rohe looking at the model of the Farnsworth House.

Film director Billy Wilder and his wife, Audrey, on their honeymoon trip to Lake Tahoe in June and July 1948. Charles and Ray Eames accompanied them. Photo: Charles Eames.

↓36 Charles and Ray Eames, Billy Wilder House model, 1950.

56 Billy Wilder House model. Interior view.

57 Billy and Audrey Wilder looking through the model of their house.

58 Cover of the catalog *The House in the Museum Garden*, MoMA, New York, 1949.

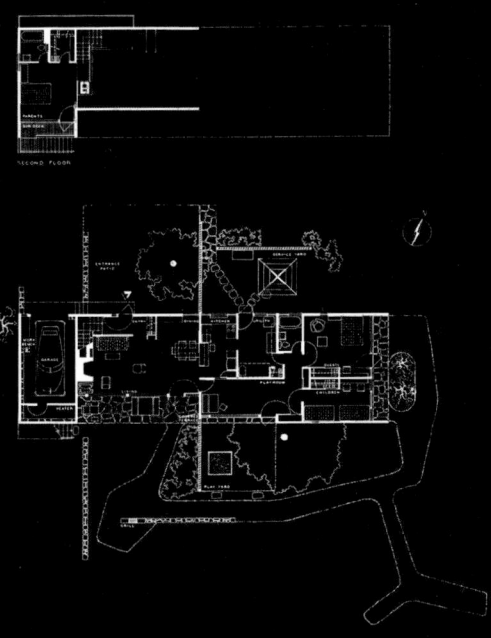

59 Marcel Breuer, House in the Museum Garden, MoMA, New York, 1949. Plan.

Marcel Breuer, House in the Museum Garden, MoMA, New York, 1949.

Installation view of the exhibition Good Design, objects on display at the Museum of Modern Art, New York, 1950.

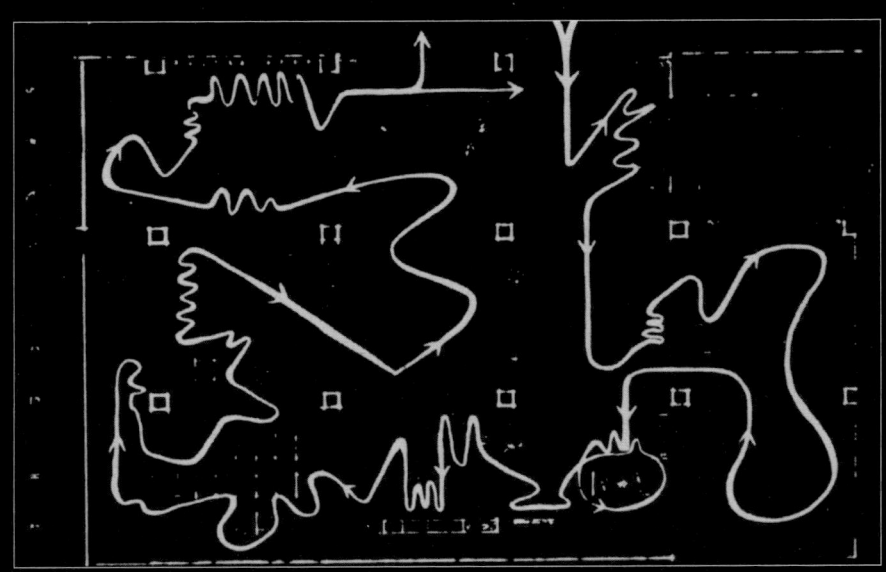

Exhibition-traffic pattern for the installation of the Good Design exhibition at the Merchandise Mart in Chicago, 1950.

MoMA Director of Design, Edgar J. Kaufmann Jr., 1951.

65 Tags for the MoMA Good Design exhibition, designed by Morton Goldsholl.

The House in the Museum Garden

Marcel Breuer *Architect*

4 West 54 Street
New York

The Cost of Construction

The architect has received fixed bids for the construction of four variations of the House in the Museum Garden from a highly reputable construction company which is prepared to build the house in Connecticut, New Jersey and southern New York State. The following prices are listed here for the information of would-be clients of the architect:

Three-bedroom house *Similar to the House in the Museum Garden (except for certain details included for exhibition purposes only)*	$17,475
Same three-bedroom house *Wall, ceiling and floor finishes of alternate materials*	15,110
Two-bedroom house: without garage and third bedroom *Wall, ceiling and floor finishes similar to the House in the Museum Garden*	12,960
Same two-bedroom house *Wall, ceiling and floor finishes of alternate materials*	10,875

These figures are based on the building costs of March 1949 in Westchester and Nassau Counties, New York, and detailed specifications are available from the architect upon request. The prices will be slightly lower if the house is built in Connecticut or northern New Jersey, and somewhat higher if built within the limits of metropolitan New York. They do not include the architect's fee nor the cost of land, landscaping and service connections from the street to the house. In view of the instability of building costs, the Museum of Modern Art can assume no responsibility for the prices quoted above.

☒☐ Brochure for the exhibition The House in the Museum Garden, MoMA, New York, 1949.
☐☒ Ibid. "Cost of Construction."

67 Marcel Breuer, House in the Museum Garden, MoMA, New York, 1949. Interior.

68 | Marcel Breuer, House in the Museum Garden, MoMA, New York, 1949. Newspaper clipping

R. Buckminster Fuller, Defense House at MoMA, press clipping, 1941.
Courtesy Estate of R. Buckminster Fuller.

70 "Road to Victory," cover of the *Bulletin of the Museum of Modern Art*, June 1942.

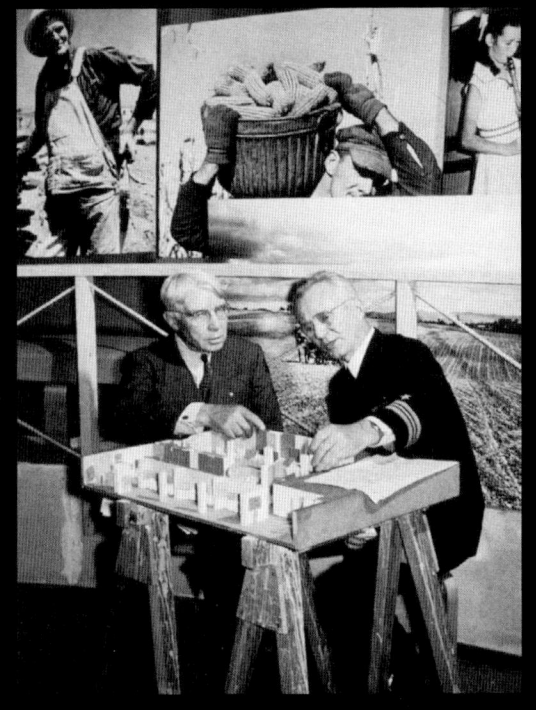

Lieutenant Commander Edward Steichen mounting the exhibition Road to Victory at MoMA, 1942.

Advertisement for Quonset Hut.
From *Architectural Record*, October 1944.

73　Pierre Chareau, Robert Motherwell Studio-House in East Hampton, New York, 1948.

the MUSEUM and the WAR

The Bulletin of
THE MUSEUM OF MODERN ART
1 VOLUME X   OCTOBER-NOVEMBER, 1942

"The Museum and the War," *Bulletin of the Museum of Modern Art*, October/November 1942.

75 Party at the MoMA Garden for the US Armed Forces.

"Power in the Pacific" and "Tomorrow's Small House," in the *Bulletin of the Museum of Modern Art*, Spring/Summer 1945.

Woman looking at the model in the exhibition Tomorrow's Small House, MoMA, 1945

78 Models of the House in the Museum Garden by Marcel Breuer show repetition of the unit.

House in the Museum Garden," MoMA, New York, 1949. Press clipping.
Note that the context of the museum has been airbrushed and replaced with clouds

Gregory Ain, Exhibition House in the Museum Garden, MoMA, New York, 1950.

Gregory Ain, Exhibition House in the Museum Garden, as published in *Woman's Home Companion*, June 1950. The context of the museum has been airbrushed to make it look like a suburban setting.

Museum Model Home Is New but Expensive

By ELEANOR ROOSEVELT.

I had my first real time off Wednesday afternoon since this past session of the United Nations General Assembly began in April. I found myself arriving a few minutes after 2 at the Museum of Modern Art.

First I went to see the model house on display in the museum garden. I don't really like it from the outside and the price seems too extravagant for most people who would live in it. If one could get the price down, there are features about it which would be tremendously attractive to a housewife who was doing her own work.

Mrs. Roosevelt.

The kitchen and laundry are well planned and compact, though I do not quite see the point of a bed in the laundry. If it is meant for a maid, few men or women servants of today would be satisfied with quarters of that kind. If it is meant for an extra guest on an overcrowded occasion, there is some point to it.

I particularly like the children's playroom with nothing but those hollow blocks which could be made into furniture and still remain toys. That, and the play yard outside, has great possibilities for further development, and the children's bedroom is adequate.

The master bedroom, bath and closet over the garage, on the opposite side of the house from the guest room, was nice in some ways but it would not allow much privacy.

The living room and dining room with the overhanging porch and the stone tables and benches outside the window, had great charm and were well and practically arranged.

The big windows everywhere add a great deal to the house because they take in the outdoors and make you feel that you are living with much more space than you actually have. The cost still seems prohibitive, however.

Afterward I saw the exhibition of prints which I enjoyed immensely and from there went up to look at the Italian exhibition of modern painters and sculptors which soon will be on view. They were all very interesting, for they reflected the effect of Mussolini, the war and the after-war period.

* * *

Making a perfect cake is easy with the correct equipment. The recipe for this fine Spice Cake with Mocha Frosting is in "Menu Makers," starting on page 62

Magazine advertisement with backdrop of the kitchen of the Exhibition House in the Museum Garden.

Cover of *McCall's* magazine, September 1949, with backdrop of the kitchen of the House in the Museum Garden designed by Marcel Breuer.

MoMA director Alfred Barr.

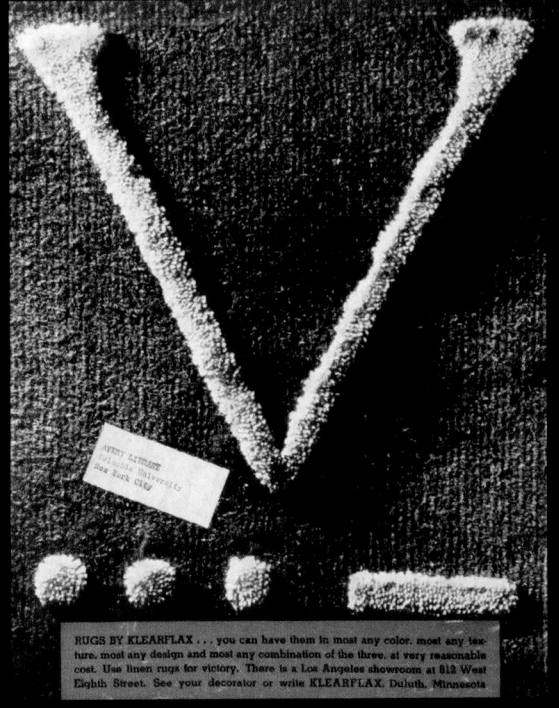

87 Advertisement in *Arts & Architecture* for Klearflax Victory rugs.

89 *Art in Progress*, 1944, exhibition catalog celebrating the fifteenth anniversary of MoMA.

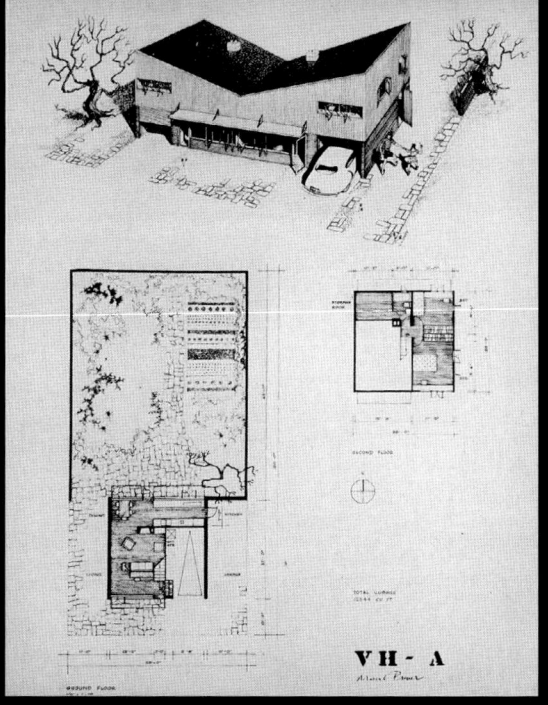

Marcel Breuer, competition entry, Designs for Postwar Living, *Arts & Architecture*, 1943.

Le Corbusier, mockup of layout of Hermès bags for *L'Esprit nouveau*, 1924.

Richard Nixon and Nikita Krushchev at the Kitchen Debate, American Exhibition in Moscow, 1959.

P. E. Bearse, rendering of Model House "Splitnik" in the American National Exhibition in Moscow, 1959. For Stanley H. Klein Architect. Courtesy of David Klein.

☒☐ Exterior Photo of the "Splitnik."
☐☒ Viewers in the bedroom of "Splitnik."
Courtesy of David Klein.

95　Watercolor rending of Leisurama House.

"Their Sheltered Honeymoon."
From *Life*, August 10, 1959.

"Containment at Home: A Cold War Family Poses in their Fallout Shelter." From *Life*, 1961.

Butler Manufacturing Corporation Grain Bin, 1930s.
Courtesy Estate of R. Buckminster Fuller.

A Typical Galvanized Steel
GRAIN BIN

With steel flooring this container is proof against fire, rodents and moisture. Its ventilator draws the excess moisture from grains such as corn, reducing the weight of the corn by 30%. Bins such as this thirty years old are still in good condition. The bin shown is 8 feet high and 10 feet in diameter. They are made in diameters up to 20 feet. In August 1939 the U.S. Government in its "Ever Normal Grainery" program ordered and received in sixty days twenty thousand 18 foot by 11 foot units and thus saved a super-bumper corn crop.

But the bin looks pretty crude as a house? Let us see what a little adaptation such as that which converts a truck into a station wagon may do.

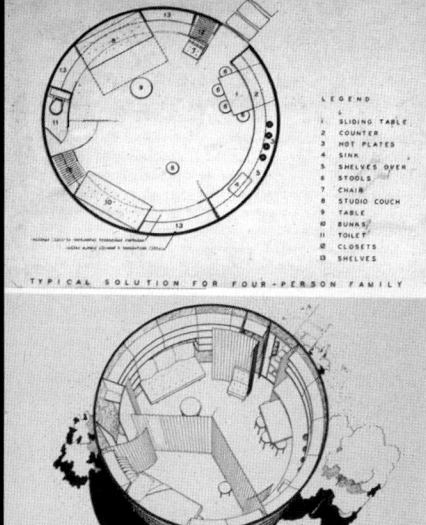

LEGEND
1. SLIDING TABLE
2. COUNTER
3. HOT PLATES
4. SINK
5. SHELVES OVER
6. STOOLS
7. CHAIR
8. STUDIO COUCH
9. TABLE
10. BUNKS
11. TOILET
12. CLOSETS
13. SHELVES

TYPICAL SOLUTION FOR FOUR-PERSON FAMILY

☒☐ Galvanized-steel bin produced by the Butler Company for the U.S. Ever Normal Grainery Program, 1939. Courtesy Butler Manufacturing Company.

☐☒ Plan of the DDU showing typical solution for four-person family. Courtesy Butler Manufacturing Company.

Dymaxion Deployment Unit, second version.
Exterior assembly of unit outside the Butler Manufacturing Company,
Kansas City, Missouri, 1940. Courtesy Estate of R. Buckminster Fuller.

Twin Dymaxion Deployment Unit installed in the garden of the Museum of Modern Art, winter 1941.

104 ↓64 Dymaxion Deployment Unit, rendering, 1940–41.

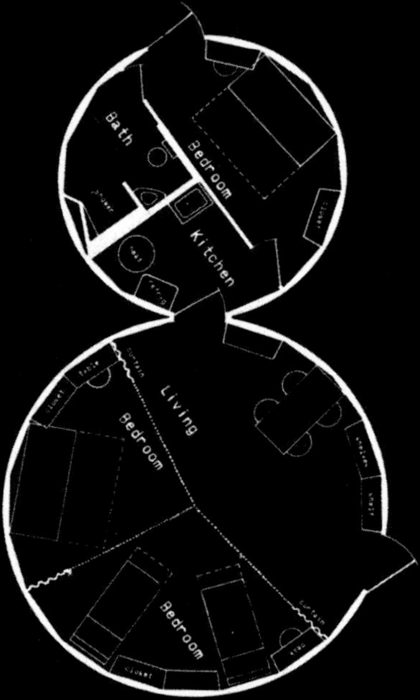

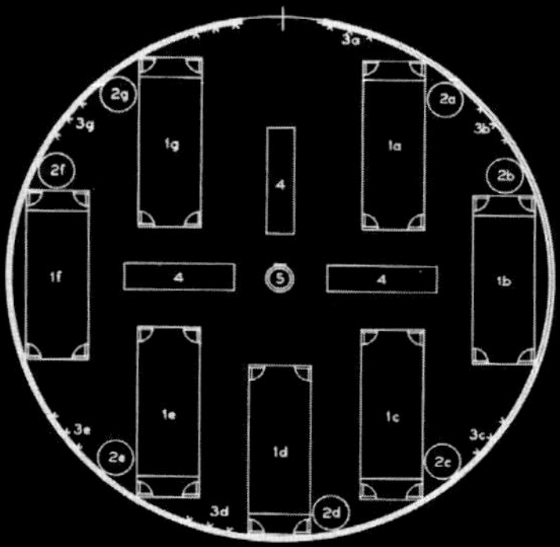

☒☐ Plan of the Twin Dymaxion Deployment Unit as installed at MoMA. Courtesy Estate of R. Buckminster Fuller.

☐☒ Plan of the Dymaxion Deployment Unit showing the unit filled with cots. Courtesy Estate of R. Buckminster Fuller.

42
71
72

Perspective of the Dymaxion Deployment Unit, 1941.
Courtesy Estate of R. Buckminster Fuller.

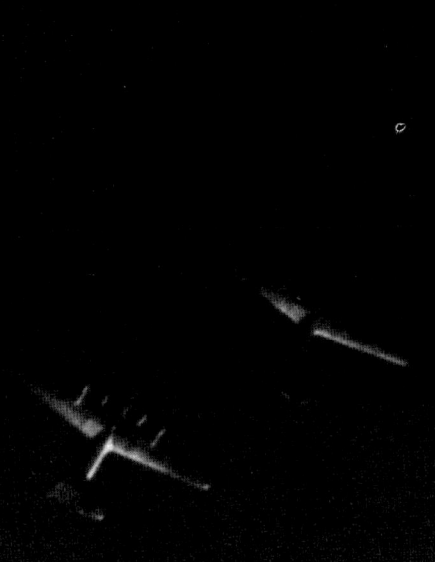

Dymaxion Deployment Unit. Photograph of the model showing the house at night with bombers overhead. Courtesy Estate of R. Buckminster Fuller.

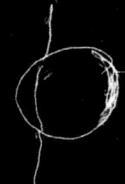

"Camouflage" and "Balistics" [sic], sketches showing the advantages of the DDU for military defense.

◼︎☐ Buckminster Fuller with model of Wichita House.
From *Fortune* 33, 1946.
☐◼︎ Buckminster Fuller, Wichita House.
From *Fortune* 33, 1946.

Wichita House. View of living room.
From *Fortune* 33, 1946.

The DDU as installed in Haynes Point Park, Washington, DC, April 1941, for study by military and government agencies. Courtesy Estate of R. Buckminster Fuller.

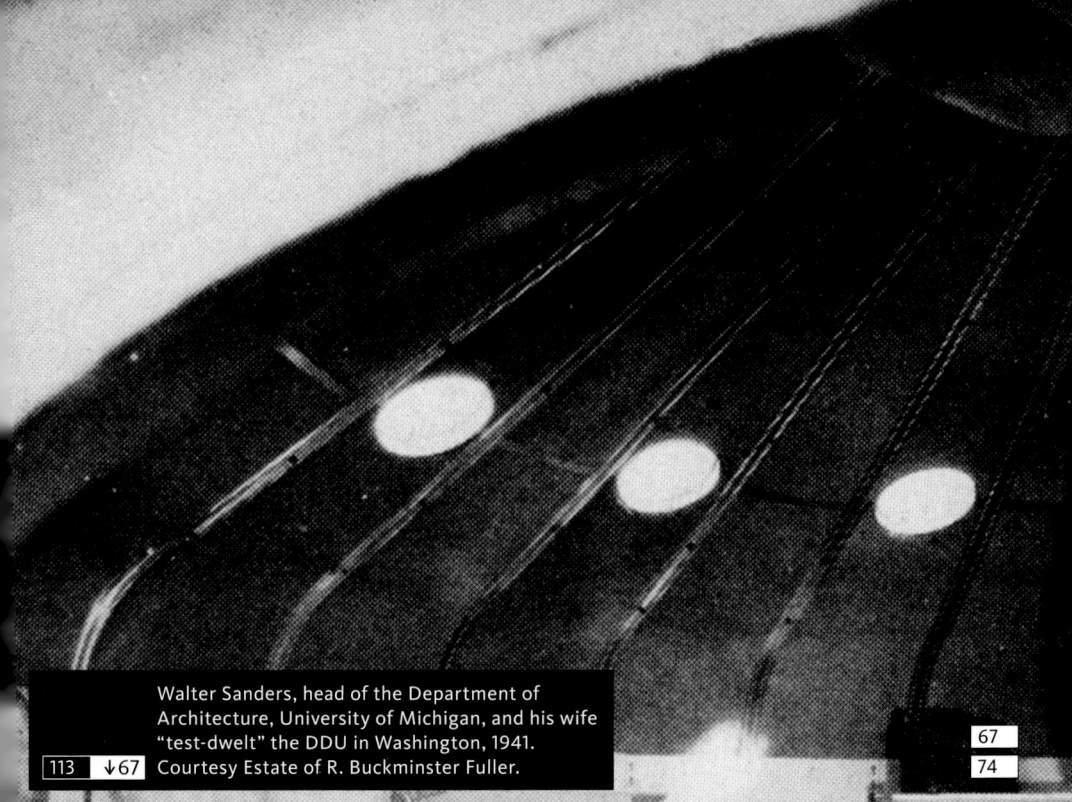

Walter Sanders, head of the Department of Architecture, University of Michigan, and his wife "test-dwelt" the DDU in Washington, 1941. Courtesy Estate of R. Buckminster Fuller.

The DDU as envisioned for civilian use, from an advertising prospectus.
From "Better Homes for Lower Incomes," Revere Copper and Brass Incorporated, Advertising Prospectus.

DDU units in the Persian Gulf during World War II.
Courtesy Estate of R. Buckminster Fuller.

"War Inspired," Buckminster Fuller with Ann Tredick, of MoMA, standing outside the DDU. Press clipping from Saint Louis *Post-Dispatch*, October 26, 1941.

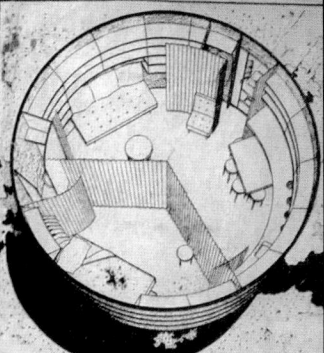

☒☐ "How to Be Comfortable Though Bombed."
From the *New Age Herald*, October 26, 1941.
☐☒ "Defense House."
From *Blade* Oct. 18, *1941*. The DDU installed at MoMA.

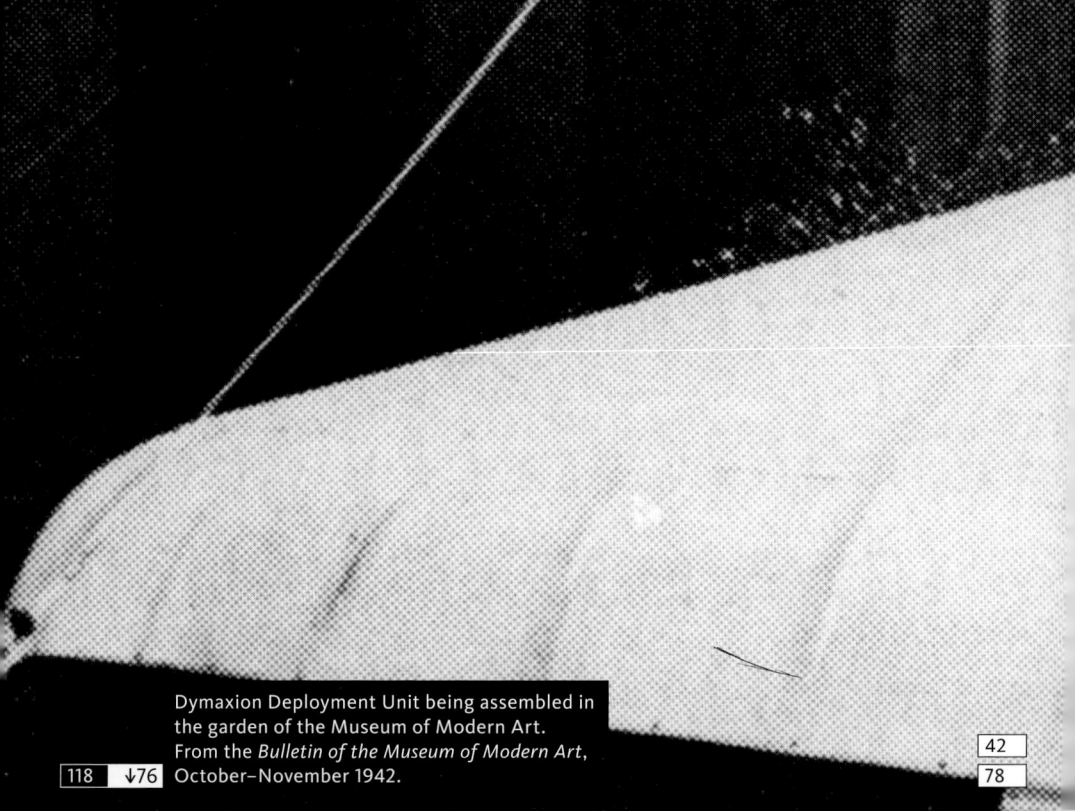

Dymaxion Deployment Unit being assembled in the garden of the Museum of Modern Art. From the *Bulletin of the Museum of Modern Art*, October–November 1942.

"Camouflage must deceive both the eye and the camera." Panel from the exhibition Camouflage for Civilian Defense, MoMA, 1942.

"Dark Fur, Pale Dress." Fashion shoot against the background of the DDU at MoMA. From *Vogue*, November 18, 1941.

122 Case Study House #8 (Eames House), shown under construction, from the back of a truck.

Case Study House #8 (Eames House). Section.
From *Arts & Architecture*, May 1949.

Charles and Ray Eames under the frame of the Case Study House #8 (Eames House) under construction.

125 Charles and Ray Eames on the steel frame of the Eames House under construction.

Charles and Ray Eames on the steel frame of the Eames House under construction, 1949. Photo: John Entenza.

Barn under construction in the USA, 1895.
Postcard from the Minnesota Historical Society

Charles and Ray Eames, sequence from *Circus*, a three-screen slide show presented as part of the Eliot Norton Lectures at Harvard University, 1970.

☒☐ Charles and Ray Eames reflected in Christmas ball.
☐☒ The Eameses posing for the previous photo.

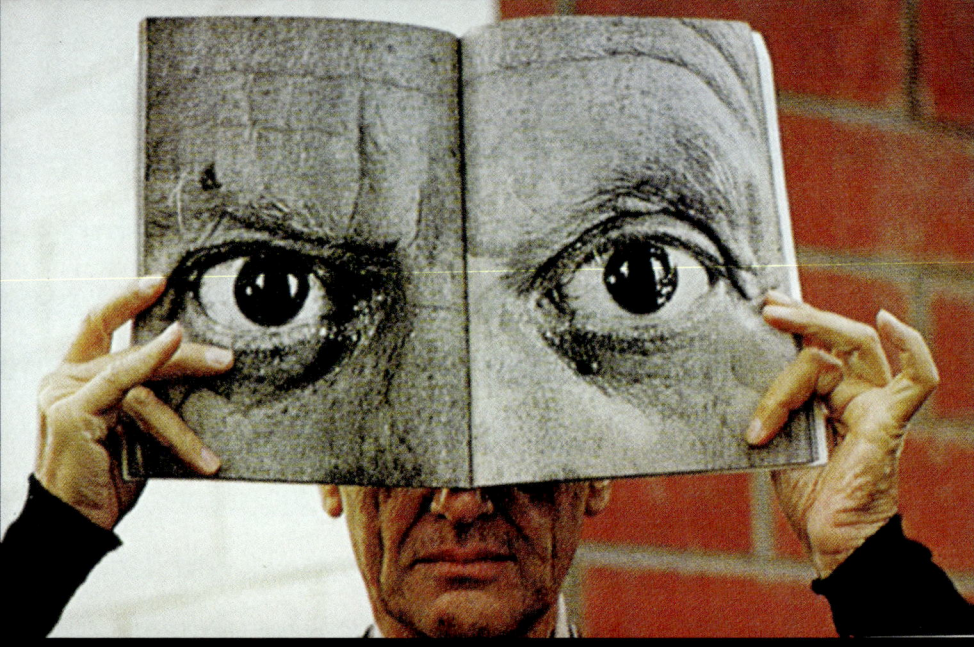

132 Charles Eames with mask.

133 Dorothy Jenkins sitting in the Eames Sofa Compact, 1954.

134 Charles and Ray Eames with model of Mathematica exhibition, 1961.

135 Eames House. Breakfast table.

Charles and Ray Eames, Building Toy.
From *Life*, July 16, 1951.

Charles and Ray Eames, Building Toy.
From *Life*, July 16, 1951.

138 Charles and Ray Eames, House of Cards, 1952.

139 Revell toy-house model.

90
96

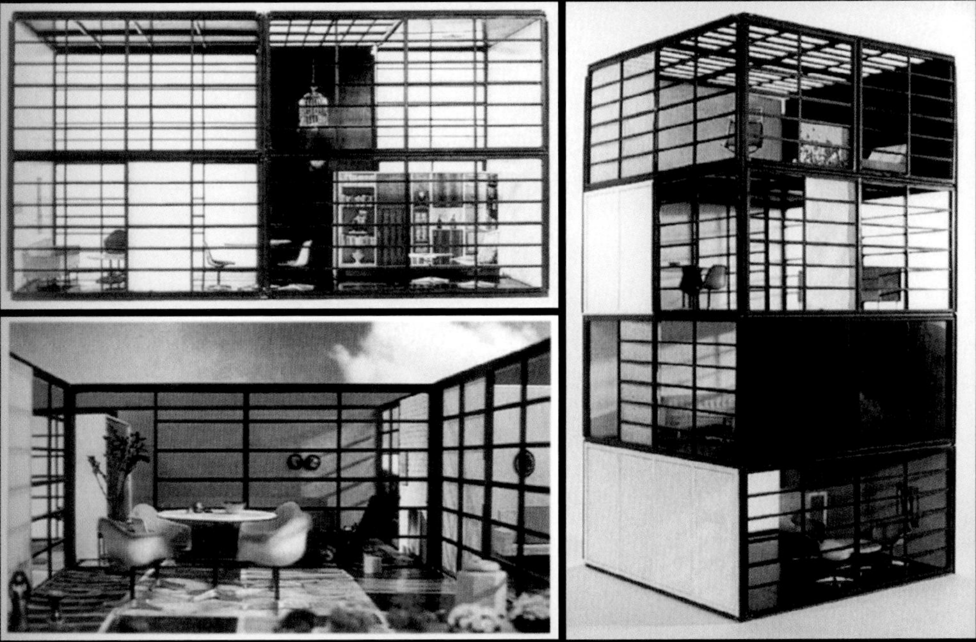

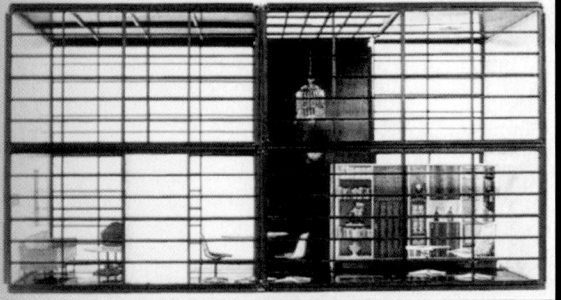

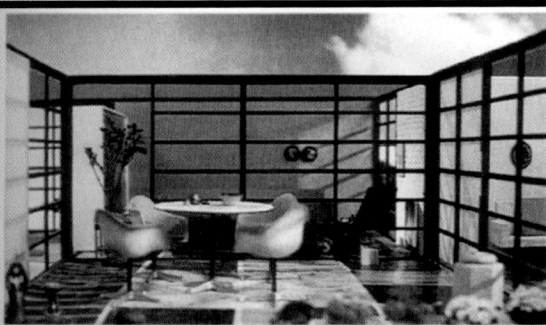

140 Charles and Ray Eames, Kwikset House.

141 Charles and Ray Eames, Kwikset House.

Living room of the Eames House, 1950.
Photo: Julius Shulman.

Charles Eames and Eero Saarinen, Case Study House #9 (Entenza House), Pacific Palisades, 1945–49.

144 Models of Case Study Houses #8 and 9. *Arts & Architecture*, March 1948.

Eames House. View of the Entrance.
Photo: Andrew Neuhart.

Charles Eames arranging driftwood in the Eames House.
From *Life* magazine.

mes House. Collectibles.

148 Cherubs hanging from staircase in Eames House.

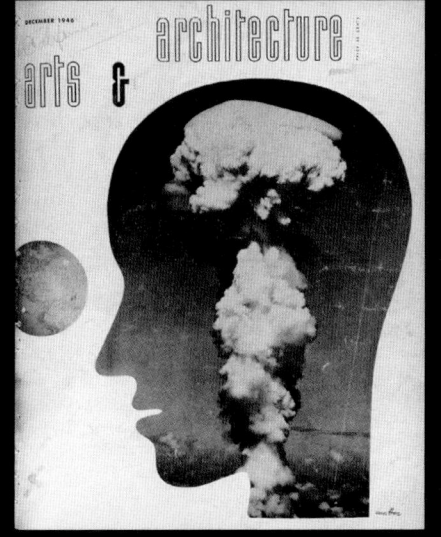

149 Cover of *Arts & Architecture*, December 1946.

150 Ray Eames and Edgar Kauffman installing Good Design exhibition at MoMA

 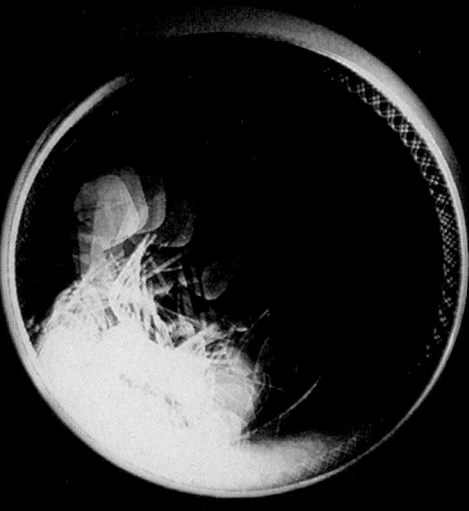

151 Tumbling drum testing durability of Eames chair, MoMA, 1945.

The Eameses' friend Doris Knox in the Eames tilted-back chair.
Multiple-exposure photograph by Herbert Matter.

"What Is a House?" Charles Eames's illustration of the activities that a house should be designed to accommodate.

Eames House. Reflections of trees through glass walls.
Photo: Charles Eames.

LIFE IN A CHINESE KITE

Standard industrial products assembled in a spacious wonderland

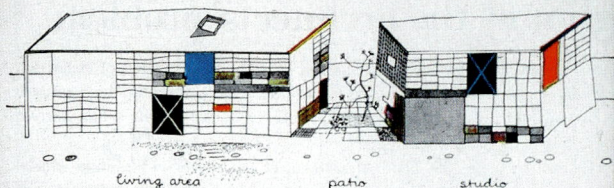

Diagram by Eames shows flexibility of frame, many ways of rearranging facade of patterns

The sparkling construction shown on these pages happens to be the place where one of America's foremost young designers and his wife are having the time of their lives. More important, it is also one of the most advanced house structures built in this country to date.

So far as Charles Eames is concerned, there is no reason why a house should not be:

▸ *Spacious— space being the greatest luxury there is;*

▸ *A sophisticated industrial product;*

▸ *And as light and airy as a suspension bridge—as skeletal as an airplane fuselage.*

Having got this straight in his own mind, Eames asked himself these questions: How cheap is space? How industrial is our building industry? How light is steel?

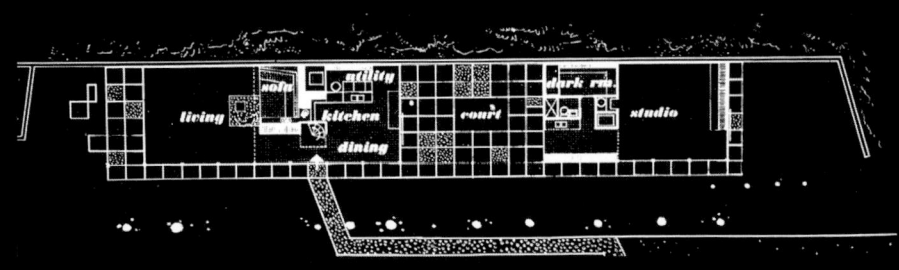

157 Eames House. Plan.

158 Eames House, in a frame from the Eameses' 16 mm film *House: After Five Years of Living*, 1955.

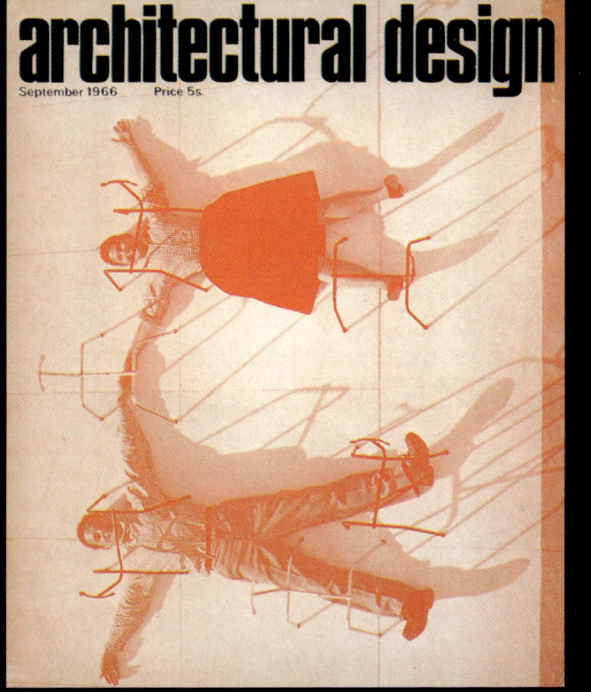

Charles and Ray Eames "pinned" by chair bases on cover of *Architectural Design*, September 1966, edited by Alison and Peter Smithson.

160 Eames mask. Giraffe.

161　Don Albinson's son Jon seated at the Eameses' child's table, 1947.

Billy Wilder in Eames lounge chair.
From *Life*.

163 ↓99 Eames plywood children's chair, 1945.

164 Ray Eames and Konrad Wachsman wearing Chinese masks.

Philippa and Miranda Dunne, daughters of screenwriter Philip Dunne, in the Eames lounge chair, 1956.

Eames plastic side chairs with cat.
From: *Look magazine*, August 7, 1956.

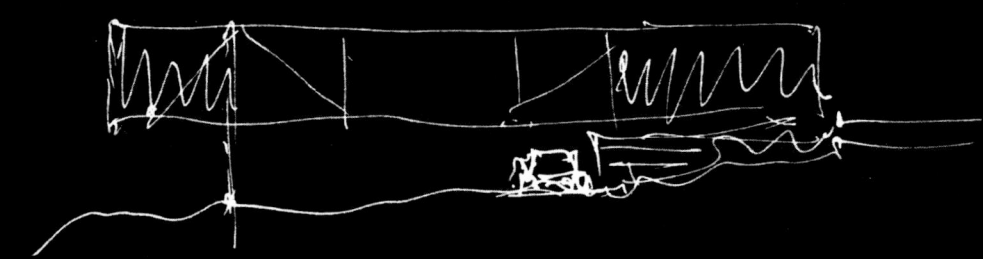

168 Mies van der Rohe, Sketch for a Glass House on a Hillside, 1934.

169 Charles and Ray Eames, model of first version of Case Study House #8, which they called "Bridge House."

Eames House, Pacific Palisades, 1949. Photo: Andrew Neuhart.

171 ↓105

Charles and Ray Eames, Eames House, Pacific Palisades, 1949. Living room. Photo: Julius Shulman.

Ray and Charles in the living room of the Eames House, 1958. Photo: Julius Shulman.

173 Eames House. Living room.

174 Eames House.

175 Stills from Le Corbusier's film *L'Architecture d'aujourd'hui.*

Details of Eames House and studio from 1949 to 1978. Photo: Charles Eames.

178-181 Charles Eames' photographs of Mies exhibition at MoMA, 1947.

182 Eames house. Reflections of trees through glass walls.

Eames House. Showing glass panel replaced with photograph of reflections.
Photo: Julius Shulman.

184 Charles and Ray Eames, Herman Miller Furniture Showroom, Beverly Hills, 1949.

185 Charles and Ray Eames, Herman Miller Furniture Showroom, Beverly Hills, 1949.

Fashion shoot in the Eames House. From *Life*, June 1954.
Le Corbusier's Weissenhofsiedlung House in a Mercedes Benz advertisement, August 1938.

☒☐ Mies van der Rohe on the building site of the Farnsworth House, 1945–51.
☐☒ Charles and Ray Eames on the steel frame of the Eames House under construction, 1949.
Photo: John Entenza.

Children Playing War in a Backyard Foxhole.
From: *Life*, November 8, 1943.

Better Homes & Gardens, July 1942. Cover.
House Beautiful, May 1945. Cover.

"Hungry Japanese Beetle Settles Down on Daisy Bud to Enjoy Meal." From *Life*, July 17, 1944.

"Kill Lawn Weeds with Weedone," advertisement.

⊠☐ "Honest, Mom, if FLIT hadn't come we would have been eating alive!" From *Life*, August 16, 1943.

☐⊠ "Man the Fleet Guns."

Fogging from Helicopter into Lawns and Forests around Hotel at Old Forge, N.Y.
From *Life*, July–August 1948.

"DDT fog swirls" around a woman as she eats a hot dog and drinks soda, Jones Beach, New York. From *Life*, July–August 1948.

"Plant Destruction by Army Worms." From *Life*, August 26, 1945.

SPEAKING OF PICTURES...

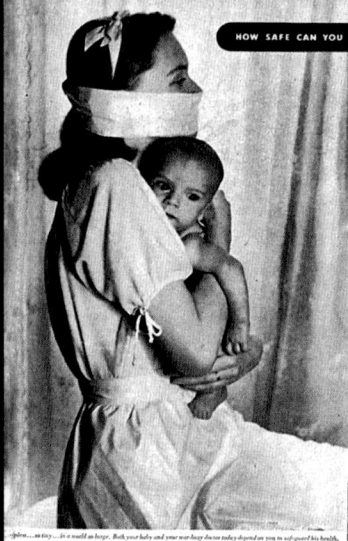

"How Safe Can You Make His War-Changed World?" advertisement for ScotTissue. From *Life*, November 6, 1944.

☒☐ Advertisement for General Electric.
From *House Beautiful,* May–June 1945, and *Life,* October 2, 1944.
☐☒ Advertisement for Poll Parrot shoes for children.

☒☐ "Victory Garden in Detroit," advertisement for Revere Copper and Brass Inc. From *Life*, March 20, 1944.
☐☒ Advertisement for a General Motors car on the lawn. From *Life*, May–June 1945.

"Family Utopia." From *Life*, November 25, 1946.

"Houseful of Plastics."
From *Life*, September 8, 1952.

☒☐ "Life Goes to a Splash Party."
From *Life*, August 12, 1940.
☐☒ "Virile Governor" demonstrating his prowess on the lawn the day before his wedding.
From *Life*, 1947.

"War Games, 1961."
Photo: Wide World.

"Sudden Death on a Suburban Lawn: A catastrophe feared by many a homeowner struck suburban East Meadow, L.I. last week when an Air Force medium bomber crashed on a lawn, set fire to a house and killed both crewmen."
From *Life*, November 14, 1955.

Aerial view of Levittown, Long Island.
Photo: Ezra Stoller.

"Shelter for Home, designed by Author Bascom, is a prefabricated plastic shell buried under three feet of earth." From *Life*, 1957.

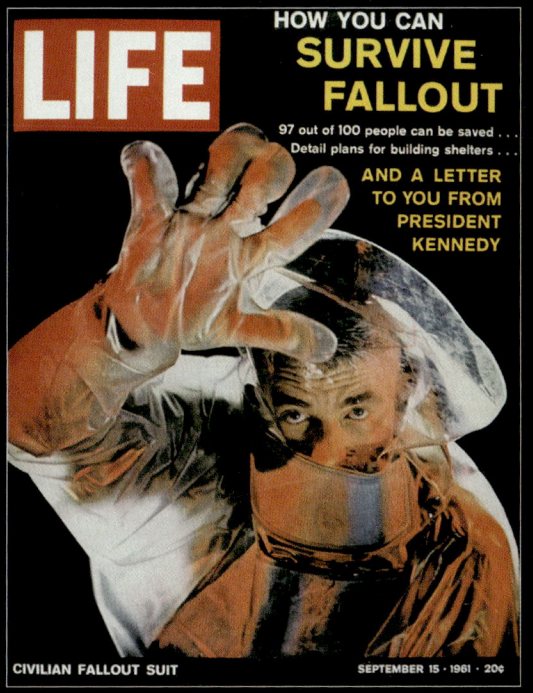

Civilian Fallout Suit.
From *Life*, September 15, 1961.

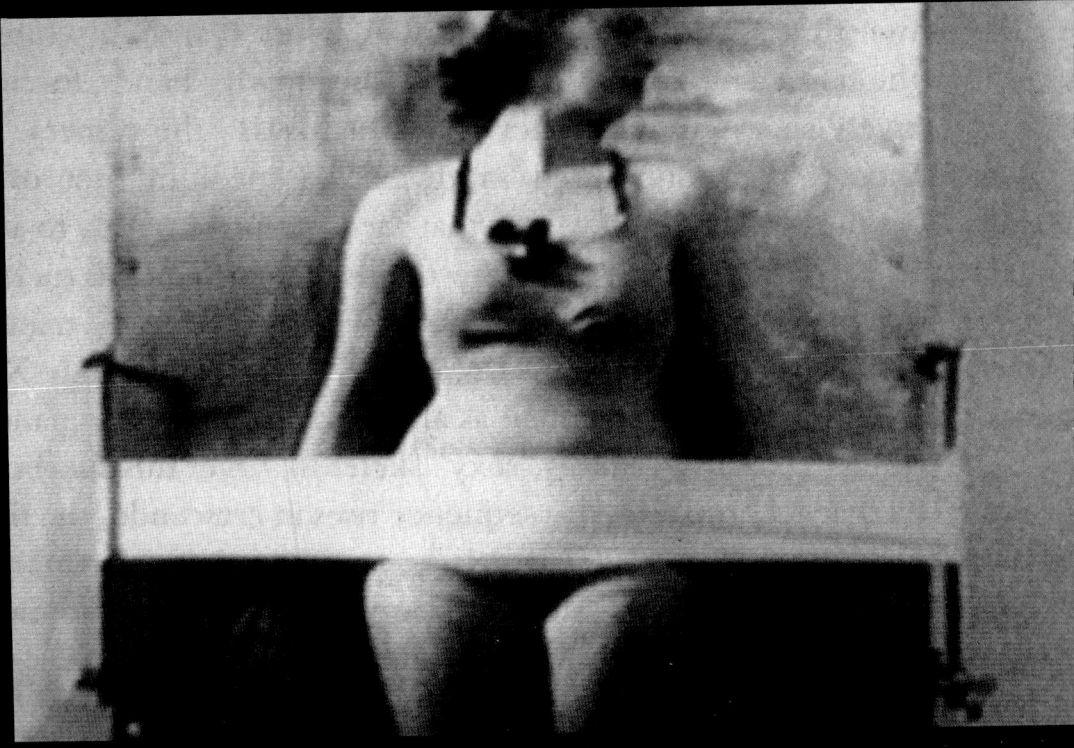

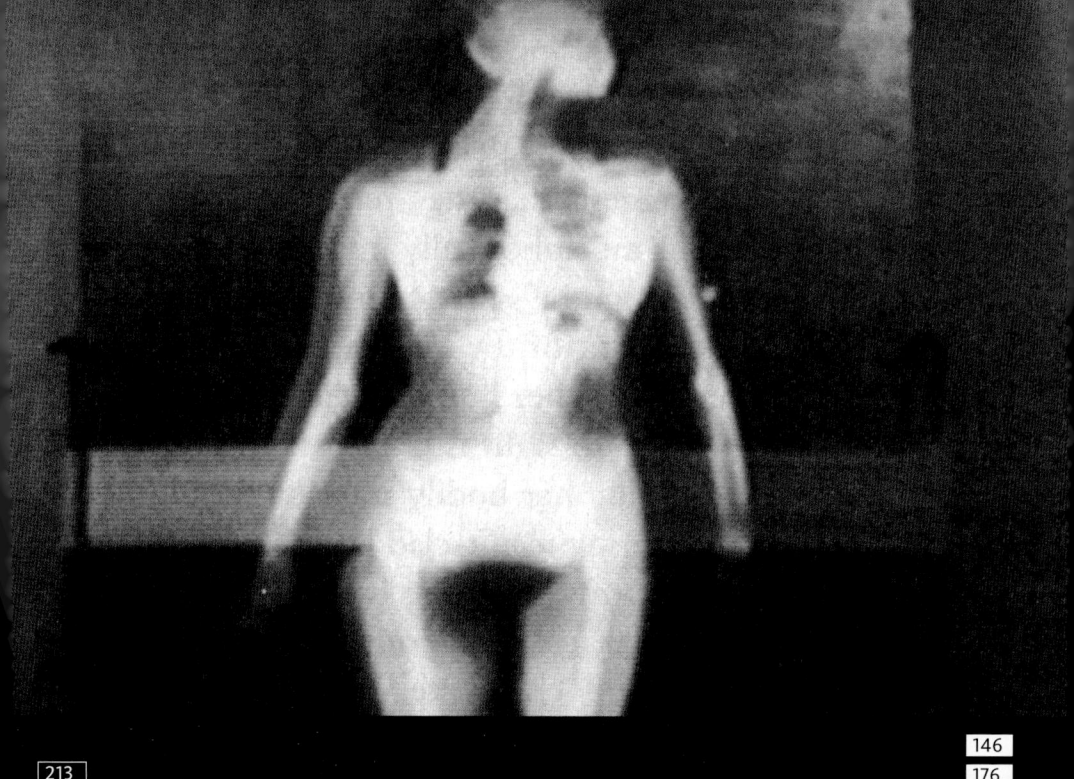

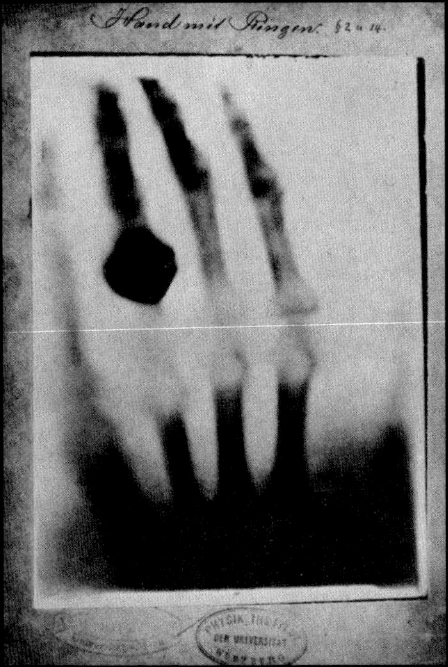

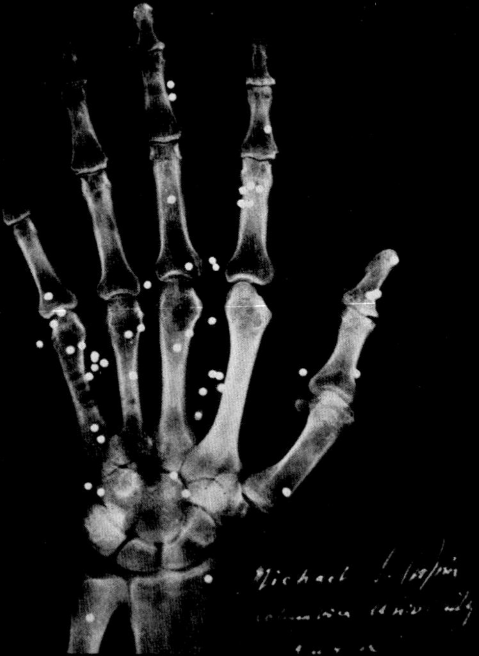

X-ray of the hand of Bertha Röntgen, 1896.
X-ray of hand with buckshot made by professor Michael Pupin, February 1896.

VICTOR ROENTGEN STAND
Model 3

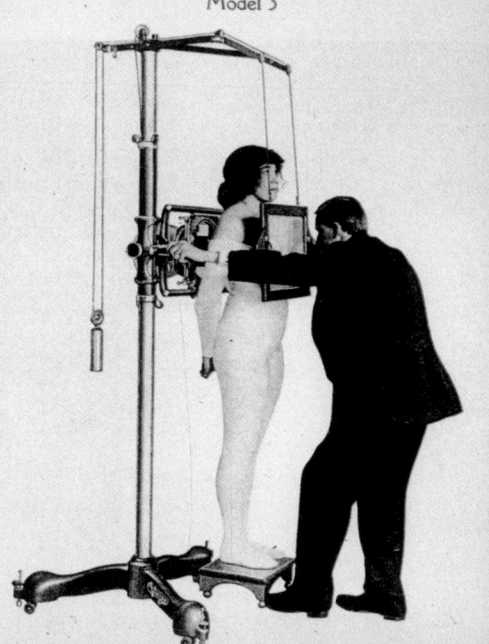

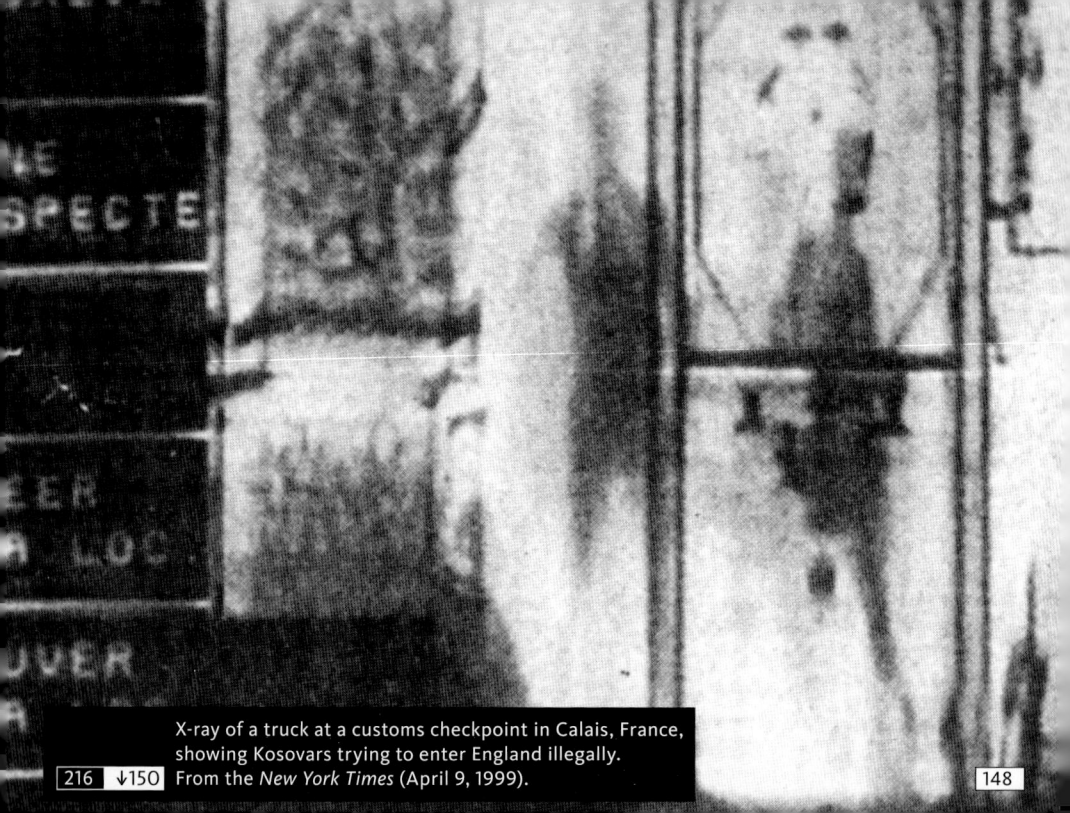

X-ray of a truck at a customs checkpoint in Calais, France, showing Kosovars trying to enter England illegally. From the *New York Times* (April 9, 1999).

Surveillance at an airport security checkpoint.
From the *New York Times*.

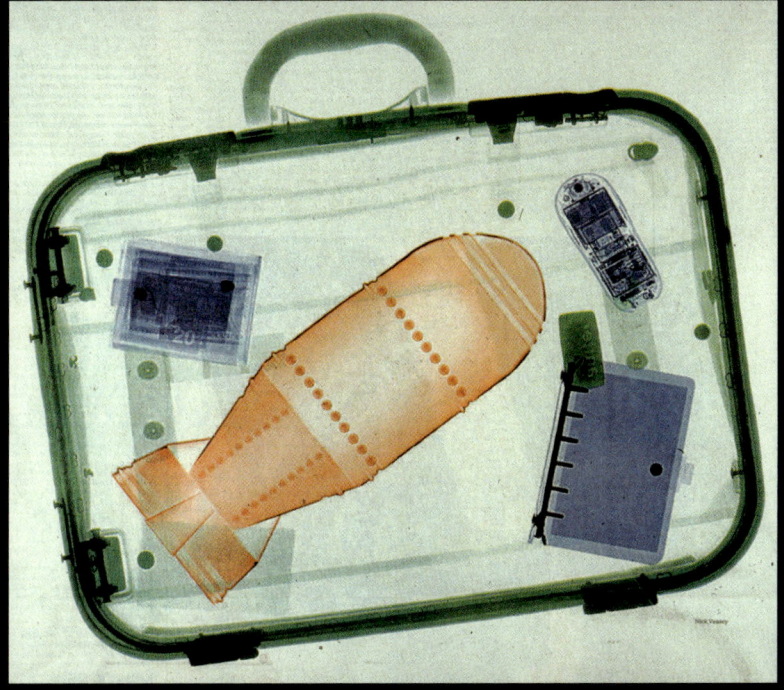

Suitcase under x-ray surveillance at an airport security checkpoint.
From the *New York Times*.

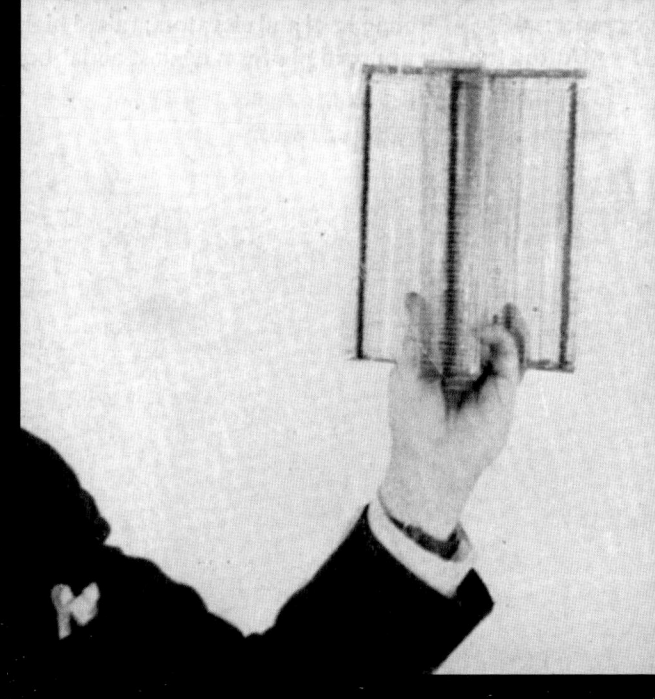

The Cartesian Skyscraper: steel and glass. Model.
Still from Pierre Chenal's film *Bâtir*, 1928.

222 Erich Mendelsohn, Schocken Store, Stuttgart, Germany, 1926–28.

George Keck, Crystal House, 1933–34, exhibited at the Chicago International Fair, 1934. A Dymaxion Car by R. Buckminster Fuller is parked in the garage.

224 Frits Peutz Architect, Schunck Glass Palace, Heerlen, The Netherlands, 1935. Night view.

225 Frits Peutz Architect, Schunck Glass Palace, Heerlen, The Netherlands, 1935. Day view.

R. Buckminster Fuller, Streamlined Dymaxion Shelter Prototype, 1932.
Courtesy Estate of R. Buckminster Fuller.

"The Biggest X-ray in the World."
From *Life*, 1946.

228 Advertisement for picture windows published in the *Saturday Evening Post*, April 26, 1958.

229 Mies van der Rohe, Farnsworth House, 1949.

Mies van der Rohe, Friedrichstrasse Skyscraper Project, Berlin, 1921. Perspective view from north. Photomontage. 140 x 100 cm, Courtesy Bauhaus Archiv Berlin.

☒☐ Mies van der Rohe, Glass Skyscraper Project, 1922. Model.
☐☒ Mies van der Rohe, Glass Skyscraper Project, 1922. Photomontage.
Courtesy Berlinische Galerie, Museum für Moderne Kunst Photographie und Architektur, Berlin, and VG Bild-Kunst.

232 Sigfried Giedion, *Befreites Wohnen: Licht, Luft, Oeffnung*, 1929. Cover.

Max Haefeli, House in Zurich, 1928, with TB convalescent on the terrace.
In Sigfried Giedion, *Befreites Wohnen*: Licht, Luft, Oeffnung, 1929.

Newspaper clipping featuring female tennis player, 1929.
In Sigfried Giedion, *Befreites Wohnen: Licht, Luft, Oeffnung*, 1929.

Woman exercising on the terrace of Richard Döcker's house in the Weissenhofsiedlung, Stuttgart, 1926–27. In Richard Döcker, *Terrassentyp*, 1929.

RICHARD DÖCKER

TERRASSEN TYP

KRANKENHAUS
ERHOLUNGSHEIM
HOTEL
BÜROHAUS
EINFAMILIENHAUS
SIEDLUNGSHAUS
MIETHAUS
UND DIE STADT

Richard Döcker, Sanatorium in Waiblingen, 1926–28.
In Richard Döcker, *Terassen Typ*, 1929.

Pfleghard and Häfeli, Sanatorium in Davos, 1907.
In Richard Döcker, *Terassentyp*, 1929.

Pfleghard and Häfeli, Sanatorium in Davos, 1907. Terrace.
239 In Richard Döcker, *Terassentyp*, 1929.

Mies van der Rohe, Tugendhat House, 1929.
Roof terrace on the upper floor with the Tugendhat children.

Living room of the Tugendhat House transformed into a gymnasium for handicapped children, 1966. Photo: Peter Blake.

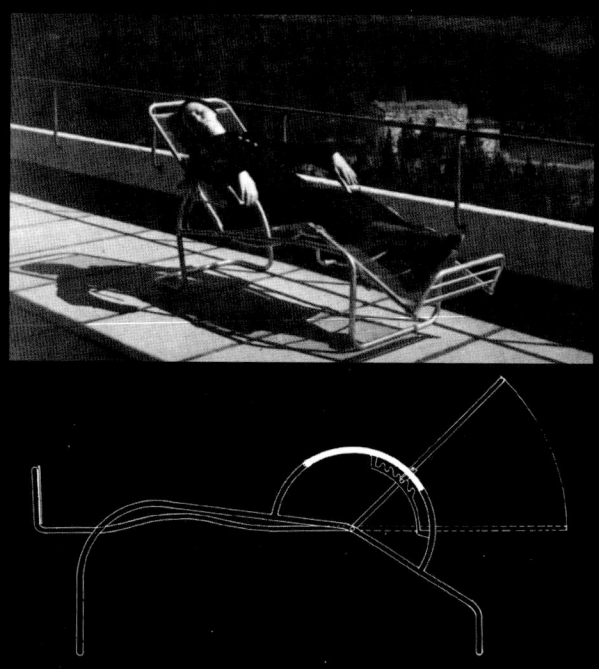

Aino Aalto in a chaise longue designed especially for the Paimio Sanatorium, 1933.
Aino and Alvar Aalto, chaise longue, 1933.

EXACT RESPIRATION

... But in the LUNG, the space which can be occupied by air is greatly increased thanks to the pulmonary alveoli which cover an estimated area of 200 M². A sheet of blood formed by the many fine links of the arterial capillaries covers an area of 150 M²; it is renewed with every contraction of the heart, that is: 70 times a minute. The heart's right ventricle pumps about 180 grams of blood into the pulmonary artery, so that every 24 hours about 20,000 Liters of it enter the lungs and will come into contact with 10,000 Liters of air ..."

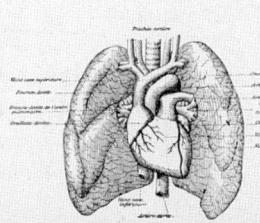

Fig. 245. — Rapports des poumons.

History. Historic Paris, tubercular Paris.

247 | Still from *L'Architecture d'aujourd'hui*, directed by Pierre Chenal with Le Corbusier, 1929.

Typical "lunger" tent on the edge of the desert near Tucson, Arizona, to house a tuberculosis patient, 1906.

Advertisement for a rest chair.

251 R. M. Schindler, Beach House for Dr. Phillip Lovell, Newport Beach, 1925–26.

252 Richard Neutra, Kahn House, San Francisco, 1940. View of terrace with chaise longue.

Richard Neutra and film star Louise Rainer in her Strathmore apartment by Neutra, Los Angeles, 1937.

The best kitchens are planned
by exasperated women

Frustrations that grow out of trying to organize your work in a poorly planned kitchen can provide the knowledge necessary for designing the best kitchen possible for you

By NANCY CRAIG

It wasn't because she was *mad* about cooking that Mrs. Helen Zundel, of Seattle, set about designing a kitchen. She wanted to spend as little time in the kitchen as possible. Between running a home and teaching dress designing at Washington University, she could never find time for everything. And she wanted to get out and serve in community projects. Being an informed woman who takes her homemaking seriously, she decided that something had to be done about her outmoded kitchen, because nothing here was ever to be found in the proper place.

What she accomplished in remodeling her kitchen proves once again that the woman who puts her mind to it can do just about anything. Without architect, without basic training, with just common sense and the help of a good carpenter, she designed with her head, and helped build with her hands, a truly beautiful and well-organized kitchen, where cooking is now a pleasure.

Mrs. Zundel had read many of the writings of Dr. Lillian Gilbreth on home management. Her basic kitchen plan was motivated by the Gilbreth philosophy of time-and-motion study. This accounts for the detailed organization of every corner and cabinet throughout the entire kitchen.

She had made a thorough analysis of what was wrong with the arrangement of the original (*Please turn the page*)

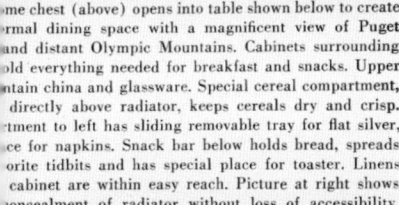
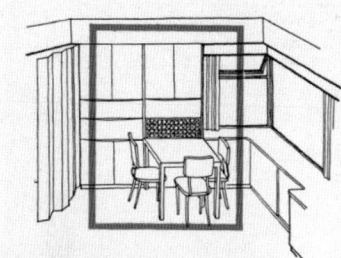

me chest (above) opens into table shown below to create rmal dining space with a magnificent view of Puget and distant Olympic Mountains. Cabinets surrounding old everything needed for breakfast and snacks. Upper ntain china and glassware. Special cereal compartment, directly above radiator, keeps cereals dry and crisp. tment to left has sliding removable tray for flat silver, ce for napkins. Snack bar below holds bread, spreads orite tidbits and has special place for toaster. Linens cabinet are within easy reach. Picture at right shows concealment of radiator without loss of accessibility.

Double-page-spread from *House Beautiful*, 1956.

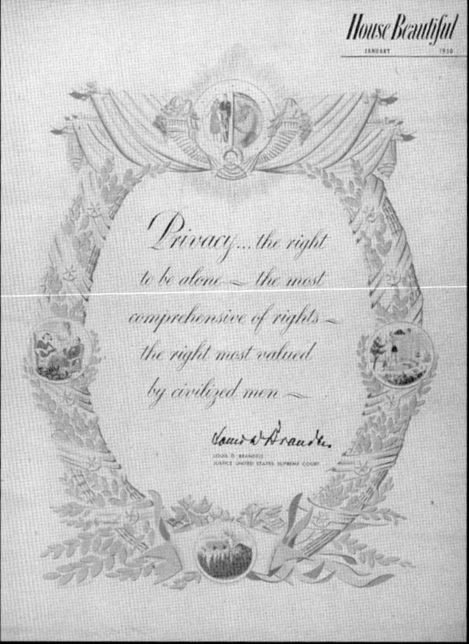

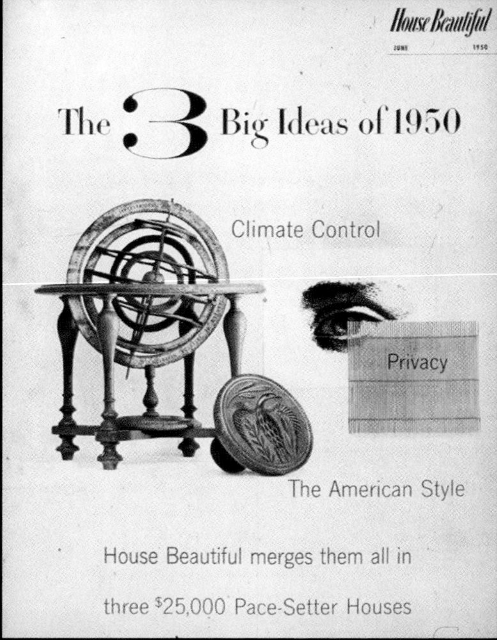

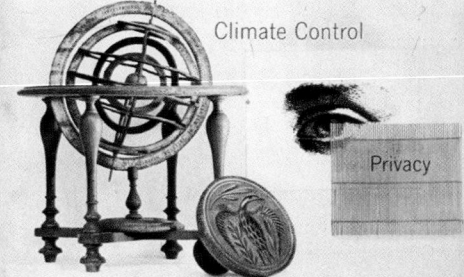

⊠□ “Privacy.” *House Beautiful* (January 1950).

256 □⊠ “The Three Big Ideas of 1950.” From *House Beautiful*, June 1950.

257 Mies van der Rohe, Farnsworth House, 1949. View of bedroom.

Dan Graham, *Alteration of a Suburban House*, 1978. Courtesy of the artist.

Mies van der Rohe speaking with King Alfonso de Borbón of Spain during the inauguration of the Barcelona Pavilion in 1929.
Photo: José Maria Sagarra.

261 Richard Neutra, Hinch House, Los Angeles, 1951.

Homes for America

D. GRAHAM

Belleplain
Brooklawn
Colonia
Colonia Manor
Fair Haven
Fair Lawn
Greenfields Village
Green Village
Plainsboro
Pleasant Grove
Pleasant Plains
Sunset Hill Garden

Garden City
Garden City Park
Greenlawn
Island Park
Levitown
Middleville
New City Park
Pine Lawn
Plainview
Plandome Manor
Pleasantside
Pleasantville

"The Serenade" - Cape Coral unit, Fla.

Each house in a development is a lightly-constructed 'shell' although this fact is often concealed by fake (half-stone) brick walls. Shells can be added or subtracted easily. The standard unit is a box or a series of boxes, sometimes contemptuously called 'pillboxes.' When the box has a sharply oblique roof it is called a Cape Cod. When it is longer than wide it is a 'ranch.' A

Set-back, Jersey City, New Jersey

The logic relating each sectioned part to the tire plan follows a systematic plan. A deve ment contains a limited, set number of ho models. For instance, Cape Coral, a Florida p ject, advertises eight different models:

A The Sonata
B The Concerto
C The Overture
D The Ballet
E The Prelude
F The Serenade
G The Noctune
H The Rhapsody

Large-scale 'tract' housing 'developments' constitute the new city. They are located everywhere. They are not particularly bound to existing communities; they fail to develop either regional characteristics or separate identity. These 'projects' date from the end of World War II when in southern California speculators or 'operative' builders adapted mass production techniques to quickly build many houses for the defense workers over-concentrated there. This 'California Method' consisted simply of determining in advance the exact amount and lengths of pieces of lumber and multiplying them by the number of standardized houses to be built. A cutting yard was set up near the site of the pro ject

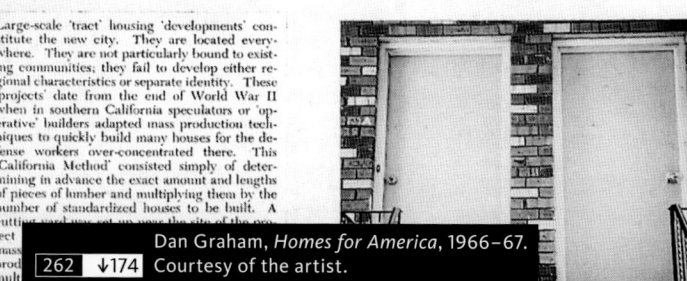

Interior of Model Home, Staten Island, N.Y.

ach block of houses is a self-contained sequence — there is no development — selected from the ssible acceptable arrangements. As an exple, if a section was to contain eight houses of ich four model types were to be used, any of se permutational possibilities could be used:

Bedroom of Model Home, S.I., N.Y.

AABBCCDD	ABCDABCD
AABBDDCC	ABDCABDC
AACCBBDD	ACBDACBD
AACCDDBB	ACDBACDB
AADDCCBB	ADBCADBC
AADDBBCC	ADCBADCB
BBAADDCC	BACDBACD
BBCCAADD	BCADBCAD
BBCCDDAA	BCDABCDA
BBDDAACC	BDACBDAC
BBDDCCAA	BDCABDCA
	CABDCABD
CCBBDDAA	CADBCADB
CCBBAADD	CBADCBAD
CCRAADD	CBDACBDA

The 8 color variables were equally distributed among the house exteriors. The first buyers were more likely to have obtained their first choice in color. Family units had to make a choice based on the available colors which also took account of both husband and wife's likes and dislikes. Adult male and female color likes and dislikes were compared in a survey of the homeowners:

'Like'

Male	Female
Skyway	Skyway Blue
Colonial Red	Lawn Green
Patio White	Nickle
Yellow Chiffon	Colonial Red
Lawn Green	Yellow Chiffon
Nickle	Patio White
Fawn	Moonstone Grey
Moonstone Grey	Fawn

Two Family Units, Staten Island, N.Y.

'Dislike'

Male   Female

'Split-Level', 'Two Home Homes', Jersey City, N.J.

'Ground Level', 'Two Home Homes', Jersey City, N.J.

Although there is perhaps some aesthetic precedence in the row houses which are indigenous to many older cities along the east coast, an built with uniform façades and set-backs ear this century, housing developments as an architectural phenomenon seem peculiarly gratuitous They exist apart from prior standards of 'goo architecture. They were not built to satisfy in dividual needs or tastes. The owner is completely tangential to the product's completion. H home isn't really possessable in the old sense; wasn't designed to 'last for generations'; and ou

Dan Graham, *Video Projection Outside of Home*, 1978.
Courtesy of the artist.

Mies van der Rohe with Herbert Greenwald.

267 Mies van der Rohe, 860-880 Lake Shore Drive Apartments, Chicago, 1948–51.

Mies van der Rohe, 860–880 Lake Shore Drive Apartments.
At night, every apartment turns into a TV set.
From *Life*, March 18, 1957.

Dan Graham, *Public Space/Two Audiences*, 1976, Venice Biennale. Courtesy of the artist.

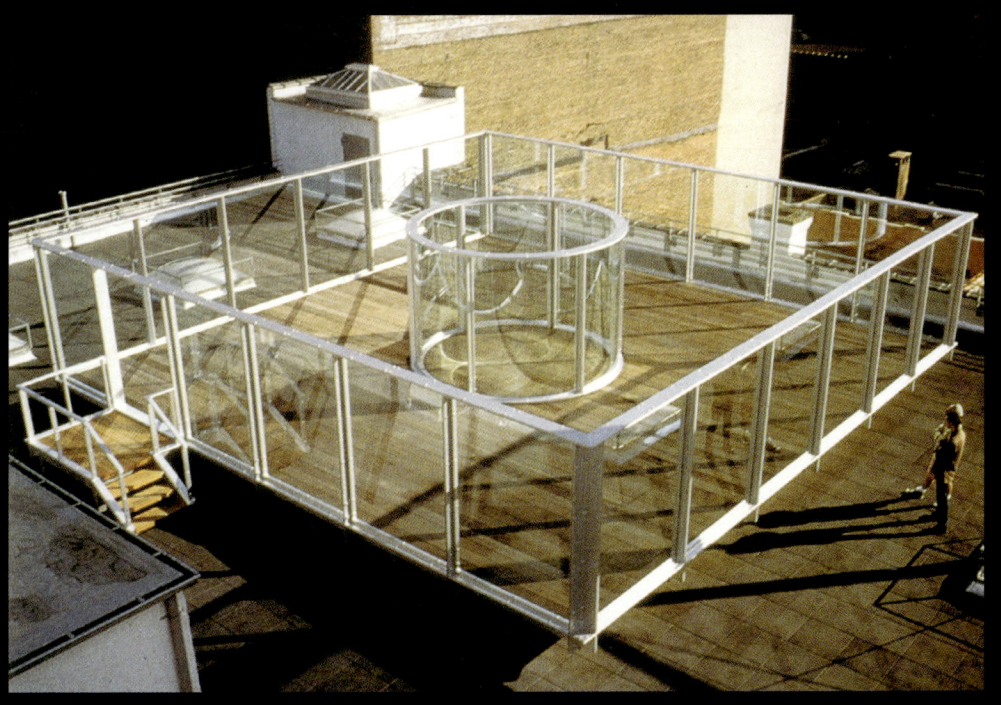

Dan Graham, *Two-Way Mirror Cylinder Inside Cube: Rooftop Urban Park Project*. Dia Art Foundation, New York. Courtesy of the artist.

Mies van der Rohe, Farnsworth House, Plano, Illinois, 1945–50.
Photo: Hedrich-Blessing, Chicago.

Philip Johnson, Glass House, New Canaan, Connecticut, 1949.
Photo: Ezra Stoller.

Philip Johnson, Glass House, New Canaan, Connecticut, 1949.
Photo: Alexandres Georges.

275 Mies van der Rohe, Farnsworth House, Plano, Illinois, 1945–50.

GLASS HOUSE

It consists of just one big room completely surrounded by scenery

BY DAY anyone can see right through the house. Vertical fiber screens, like those at left and right, shield the interior from the sun's heat. At left: Johnson.

As director of the Museum of Modern Art's architectural department, Philip C. Johnson likes to build extremely modern houses and try them out on himself. His latest experiment, until the chilly recency near New Canaan, Conn., is the current construction piece of U.S. architecture. It consists of two striking structures, one almost entirely transparent, the other almost completely opaque (p. 96). The first is a 32x56-foot building of only one room complexly walled by glass. Kitchen, dining, sleeping and living areas are separated merely by cabinets which stop short of the 10½-foot ceiling or by such subtle demarcations as furniture placement or a rug. Only the bath, in a 10-foot-wide brick cylinder, is enclosed. The second building, 100 feet away and virtually windowless, has two guest bedrooms, a picture gallery and a study where Johnson can enjoy the contrast of feeling thoroughly walled in.

After living transparently for nine months, Johnson regards his experiment as a success. On 13 acres he has privacy. Heat loss through the plate glass is compensated for by radiant heat. Johnson claims the weather's "feel" is transmitting; from his fireside a storm is exciting, new snow a lovely miracle. For friends who joke about the perils of stone-throwing, he has an answer: "People don't throw stones at shop windows. Why should they throw them at mine?"

BY NIGHT floodlights illuminate trees outside. Low kitchen cabinets are at left, bath cylinder in center, "bedroom" at right. Dining area is beyond kitchen.

"Glass House."
From *Life*, September 26, 1949.

277 Bruno Taut, Glashaus under construction, late March/early April 1914.

Philip Johnson, Glass House, New Canaan, Connecticut, 1949. Photo: Arnold Newman.

280 Mies van der Rohe, Farnsworth House. Model, 1947.

Philip Johnson, Glass House. Scheme XII, 1947, model.

The television set at the center.
From *Life* magazine. Photo: Thomas McAvoy.

283 Advertisement for Dumont TV set.

Philip Johnson, Glass House, New Canaan, Connecticut, 1949. Interior view. Photo: Ezra Stoller.

Philip Johnson, Glass House, New Canaan, Connecticut, 1949. Guesthouse and pool.
Photo: Ezra Stoller.

Philip Johnson, Glass House, New Canaan, Connecticut, 1949. Guesthouse. From *Life*, September 26, 1949.

Philip Johnson in the guesthouse of the Glass House, New Canaan, Connecticut, 1949. From *Life*, September, 1949.

Mies van der Rohe, Farnsworth House in flood conditions, 1950–51. Courtesy of Edward Duckett.

Page from *House and Garden* featuring Mies van der Rohe's Farnsworth House, February 1952.

290 Philip Johnson, Glass House, New Canaan, Connecticut, 1949.

291 Philip Johnson, New Canaan, Connecticut, Glass House.

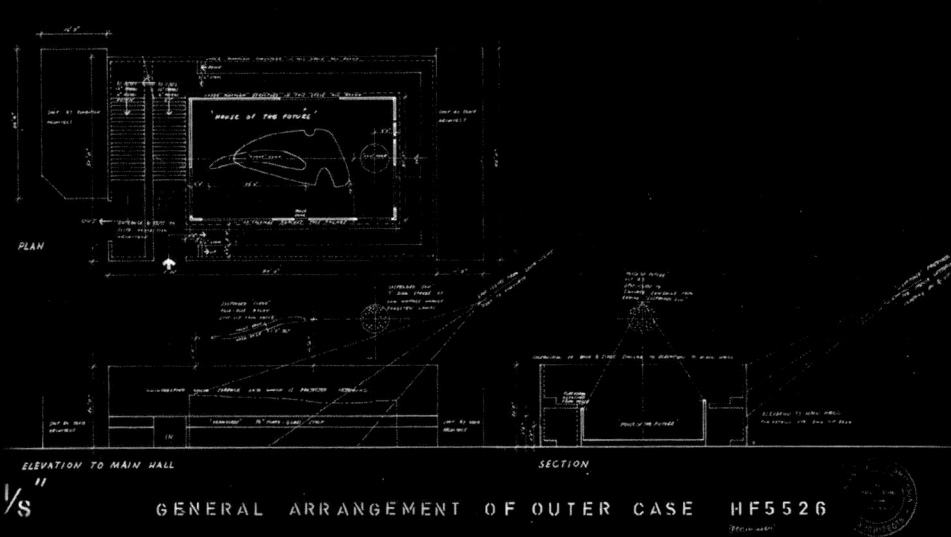

Alison and Peter Smithson, Drawing of the Outer Case of the House of the Future, *Daily Mail Ideal Home Exhibition*, London, 1956.

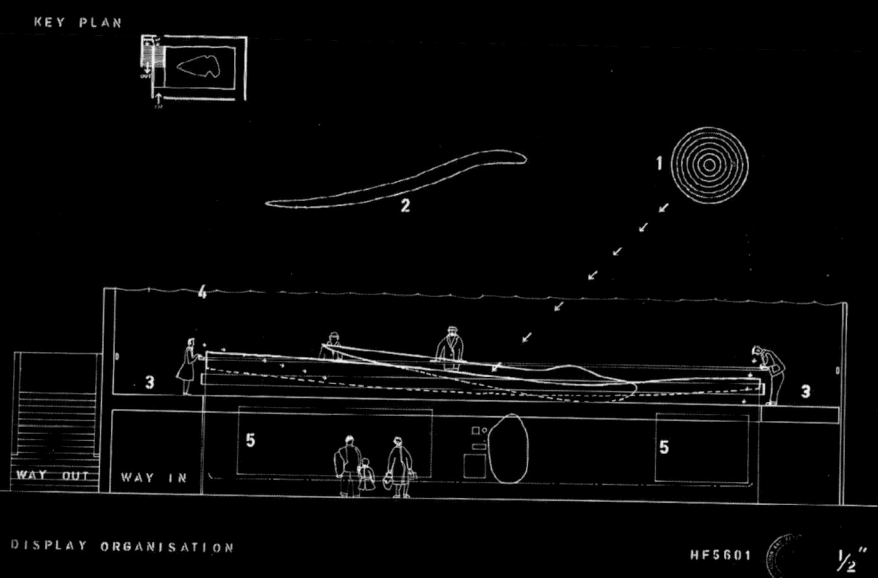

Alison and Peter Smithson, House of the Future. Section through the outer case showing the proposed artificial sun and floating cloud, 1956. "Key: (1) sun, (2) cloud, (3) upper viewing gallery, (4) velarium, (5) viewing windows."

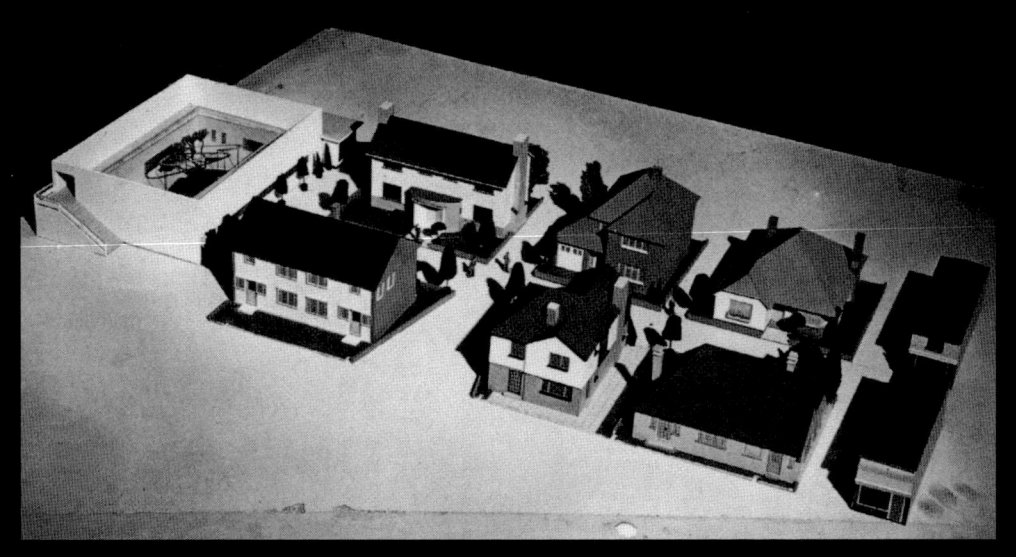

Alison and Peter Smithson, Model of the House of the Future as part of the layout of traditional houses.

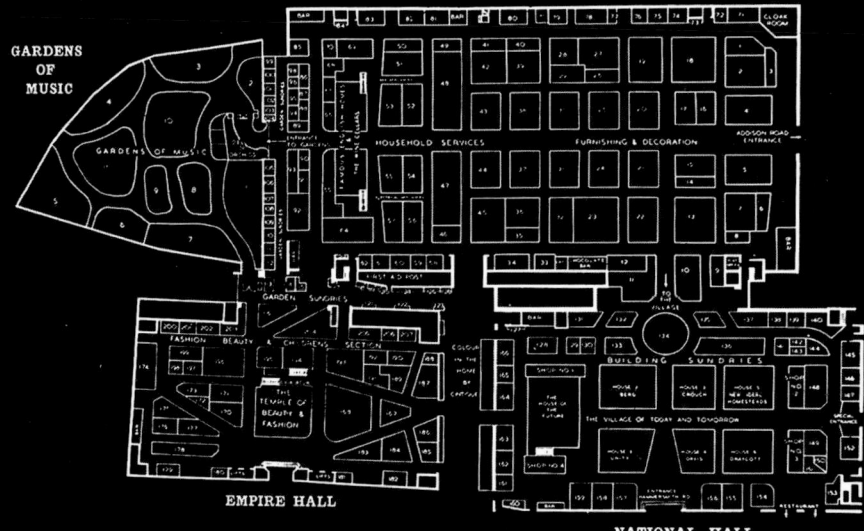

Ground plan of Olympia Exhibition Hall in London showing location of the Smithsons' House of the Future.

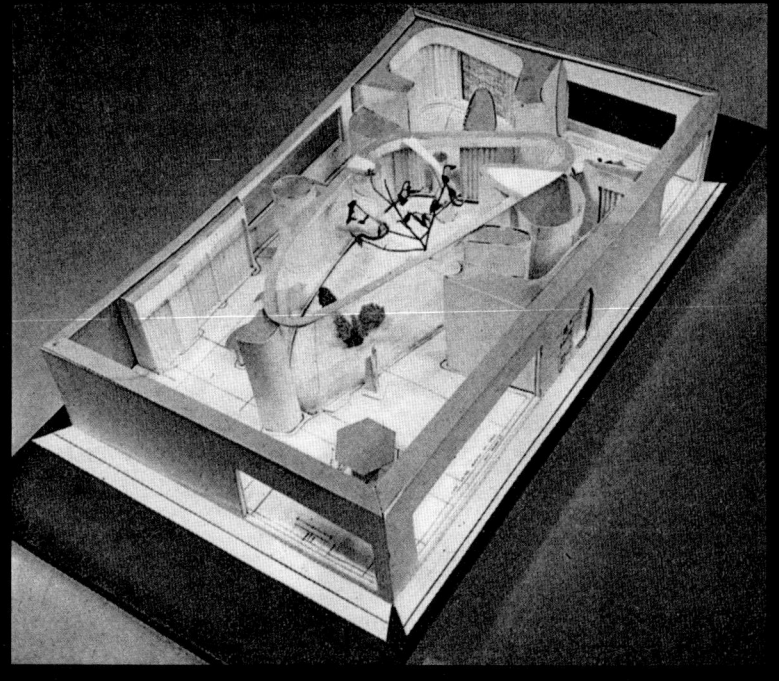

Alison and Peter Smithson, model of the House of the Future, 1956. View from above with the warped roof removed.

Alison and Peter Smithson, House of the Future.
Living room with hexagonal table in raised position, serving trolley, Pogo, Petal, and Egg Chairs.
297 Back-projection television on the wall.

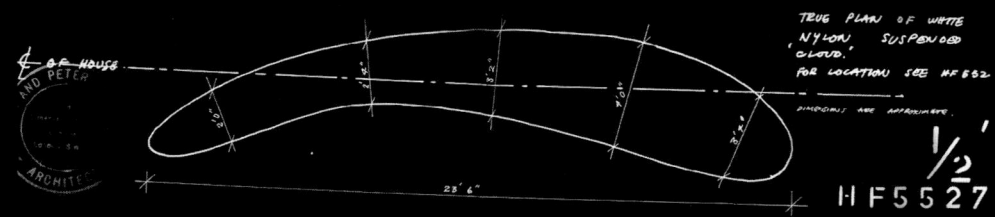

Alison and Peter Smithson, plan of white nylon suspended "cloud" for the House of the Future. Unrealized.

Alison Smithson, prototype of the upper section of the Tulip Chair, fiberglass-reinforced polyester molding, 1956. Photo: Peter Smithson.

300 House of the Future. View from patio onto bath.

301 House of the Future. View from bedroom onto patio.

Prepackaged food on the kitchen counter of the House of the Future. Photo: C.O.I.D., 1956.

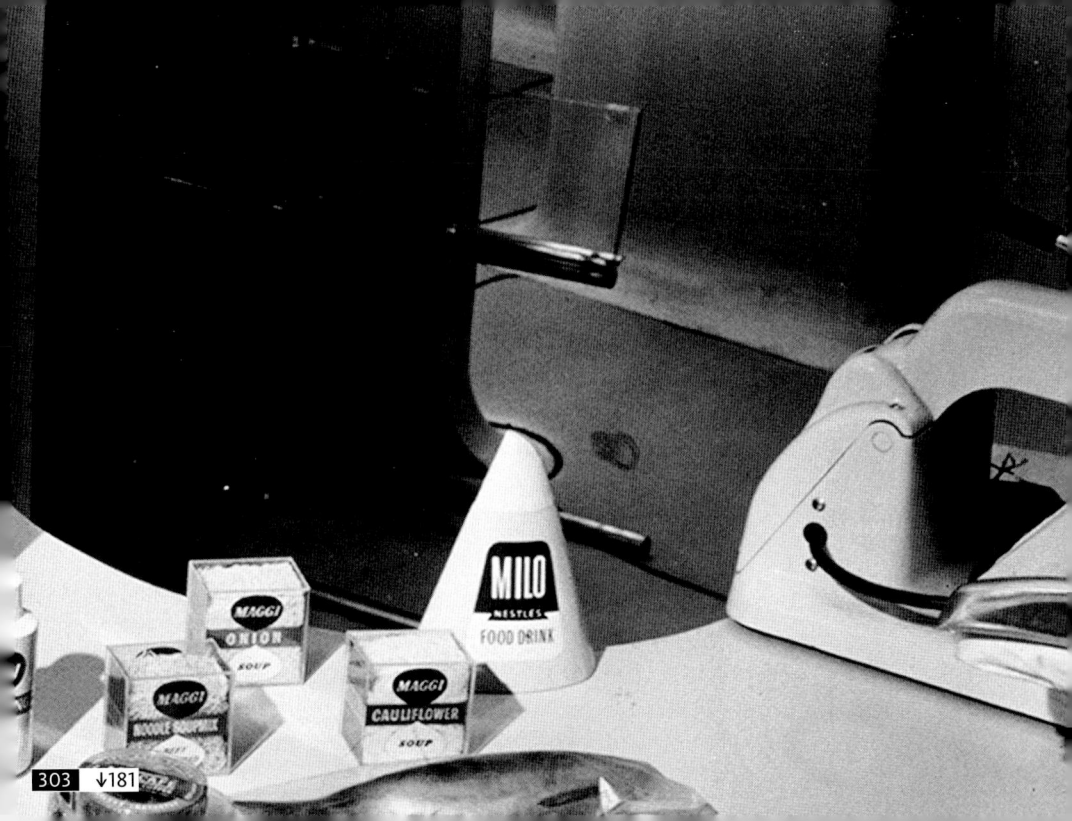

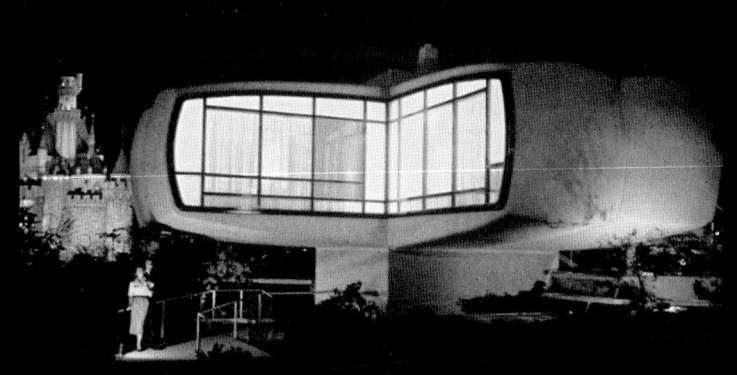

304 Monsanto House of the Future, Disneyland, 1956.

305 Tupperware products displayed on a highway.

Construction of the House of the Future in the Daily Mail Ideal Homes Exhibition, London, 1956. The forms were simulated in plywood and the inside face later painted. The inside color was meant to be faunish (based on the stone color in the medieval painting *The Garden of Paradise*). Photo: Sam Lambert.

Peter Smithson, "Fougasse" layout of a neighborhood of "Houses of the Future," with a density of seventy houses to an acre, 1955. "A 'fougasse' was a type of French bread with holes in it, shaped like a hand and met on '50s expeditions into continental Europe."

Alison and Peter Smithson, Parallel of Life and Art exhibition at ICA, London, 1953.
Photo: Nigel Henderson.

Alison and Peter Smithson, Patio and Pavilion, This Is Tomorrow exhibition, Whitechapel Art Gallery, London, 1956.
Photo: Nigel Henderson.

Airstream Land Yacht. "Caravans properly used become objects in a more or less uninhabited landscape—not sub-standard dwellings." From Alison and Peter Smithson, *Ordinariness and Light*, 1970.

Advertisement showing car interior, 1955. "The caravan is as comfortable as the latest car model and, like the car, it represents a new freedom." From Alison and Peter Smithson, *Ordinariness and Light*, 1970.

312 Le Corbusier and Pierre Jeanneret, Villa Stein–De Monzie, 1927. Photograph of entrance, with Le Corbusier's Voisin car.

Alison and Peter Smithson, Upper Lawn Pavilion, Fonthill, 1962.
View form the road side with Citroën ID.
From AS in DS, 1983. Photo: Peter Smithson

314 Covers of Alison Smithson book *AS in DS*, Delft, 1983.

The Smithsons' Citroën DS Safari covered in snow, in front of Cato Lodge, their house in London, 1978. From *AS in DS*.

Peter Smithson leaving his Volkswagen Beetle on his way to the installation of the House of the Future, 1956.

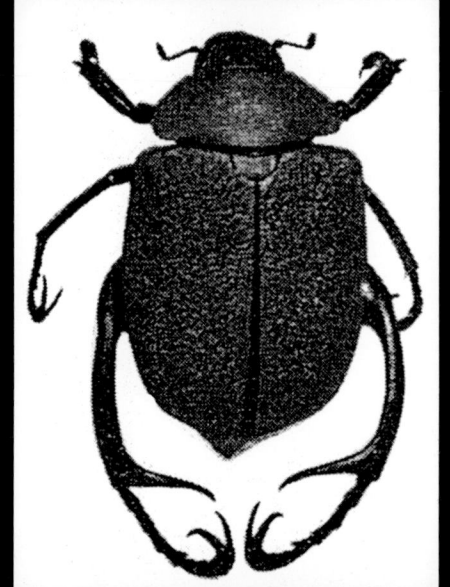

Image of a beetle used by Reyner Banham in his article on the House of the Future, "Things to Come." Banham: "Looking down into the bathroom, one sees the discontinuous, jointed structure of the house, designed in analogy with jointed, moulded natural structures like a beetle's wing cases."

318 Alison and Peter Smithson in their studio at Cato Lodge, 1973.

Alison and Peter Smithson in Patio and Pavilion, 1956.

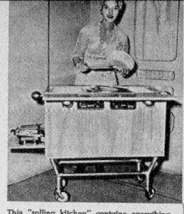

rays. Almost everything in the house is plastic, including the translucent walls and chairs—practically the only mobile equipment (everything else is built in). Even the eggs in the kitchen come in little plastic bags.

All electric power is drawn from a nearby atomic power station. The house is entirely air-conditioned and warmed by radiant heating in the floor.

A short-wave transmitter with push buttons controls all electronic equipment. We're sure you'll be interested to know that the shower stall has jets of warm air for drying and the sunken bathtub rinses itself with detergent. No bathtub rings left for Mother. *

This "rolling kitchen" contains everything necessary to serve complete meal anywhere at all in "cave-like" doorless house.

Sink is glass-reinforced plastic, has a foot control, dispenses any degree water.

Work table in utility room has sink, tiny bird water cup, built-in sewing machine.

Plastic niches surround dressing room mirror. The entire unit can be concealed behind a flexible plastic draw curtain.

Food preserved by bombardment of gamma rays can be stacked on open shelves of cupboard. Even eggs are plastic-bagged.

Sunken plastic bath is thermostatically controlled. Man stands near cylindrical shower with air jets for drying.

Blanketless bed (it has single heated nylon sheet) sinks into floor when not in use.

"This Is a House?"
House of the Future in newspaper clippings, March 1956.

Dressing room of the House of the Future with Saddle Chair and two "inhabitants," 1956. Photo: *Daily Mail*.

Bedroom of the House of the Future with two couples of "inhabitants" and a lace nightdress laid out on the bed.

House of the Future. Dining room with a couple of "inhabitants." The dice in the man's hand is a remote control. Mobile food serving trolley to the left.

Bedroom of the House of the Future with "inhabitants." The island bed has its base molded into the floor. The mattress and headrest are latex foam covered with nylon, and the bedclothes consist of one easily washable nylon sheet. In one corner of the room is a portable Electrostatic dust collector. Photo and caption text: *Daily Mail*.

House of the Future. Entrance door with extract grill to remove dirt from shoes before entering. Photo: C.O.I.D., 1956.

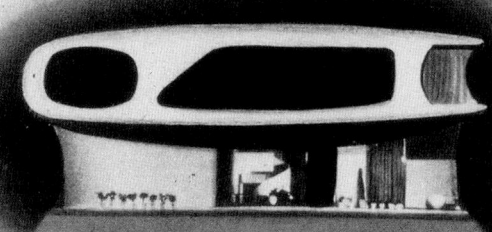

328 House of the Future. Bedroom.

329 Alison and Peter Smithson, House of the Future, 1956. Drawing of furnished plan at lower level. 218

330 Hugh Hefner with model of Playboy Club Hotel to be built in Los Angeles, 1962.

331 Playmate on Saarinen Womb Chair, 1959.

Look! We're in Wonderland

AIL, Monday, March 12, 1956

Clift children see ...ase of magic ...ch will welcome ...em as grown-ups

By BARBARA and HUGH CLIFT

ELL, here we are at the *Daily Mail* Ideal Home Exhibition, in London, and we ...ve just spent hours and hours in the House ... the Future which we have heard so much ...bout, and which we now know everything ...about.

...eally it was a bit of luck that we could come. You see, the older pupils in our school at Chalfont St. Peter were doing an examination, and we were given the day off to get us out of the way.

And we remembered the House ... the Future, and so we ...am... to London.

...r it shall be grown up by ...e time everyone has a house ...e that, because we are nine ...d seven now and the house is ...signed for 1980.

...t we are not sure that we are ...oking forward to living in a ...House of the Future, even if it is marvellous as everyone says.

...e prefer a house in the country ...ike Flint Cottage, where we live.

...ell, we went into the living-room of the House of the Future first and it was rather weird, and we felt a bit lost, especially when someone said that we were standing on the table.

The table turned out to be great fun. It comes out of the floor...

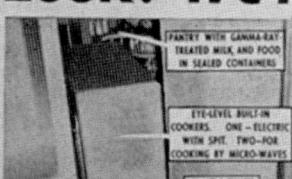

"Look! We're in Wonderland."
From the *Daily Mail*, March 12, 1956.

House of the Future, 1956. Living room with hexagonal table down, flush with floor.
Photo: John McCann.

"Housewife's Dream—It May Be 1984."
From the *News Chronicle*, March 6, 1956.

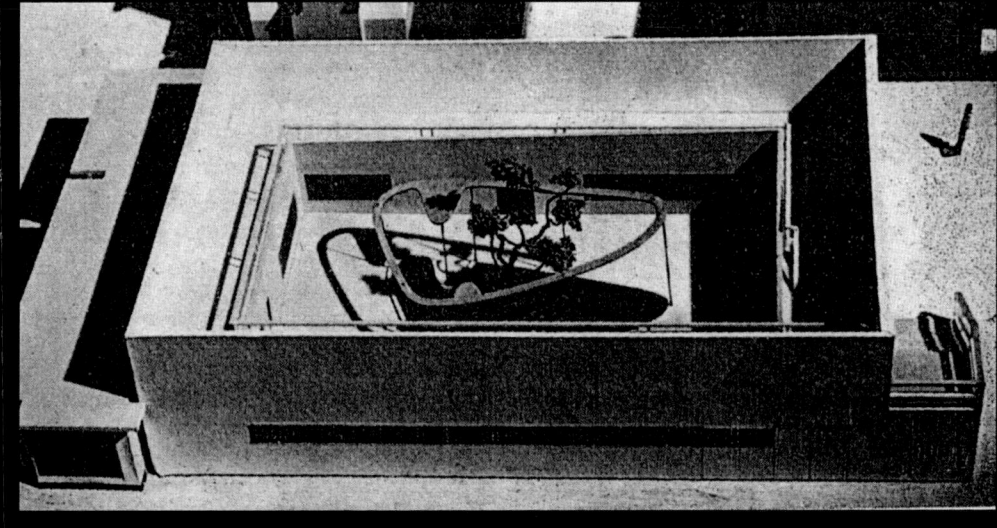

Alison and Peter Smithson, House of the Future, 1956.
335 Model of the outer case.

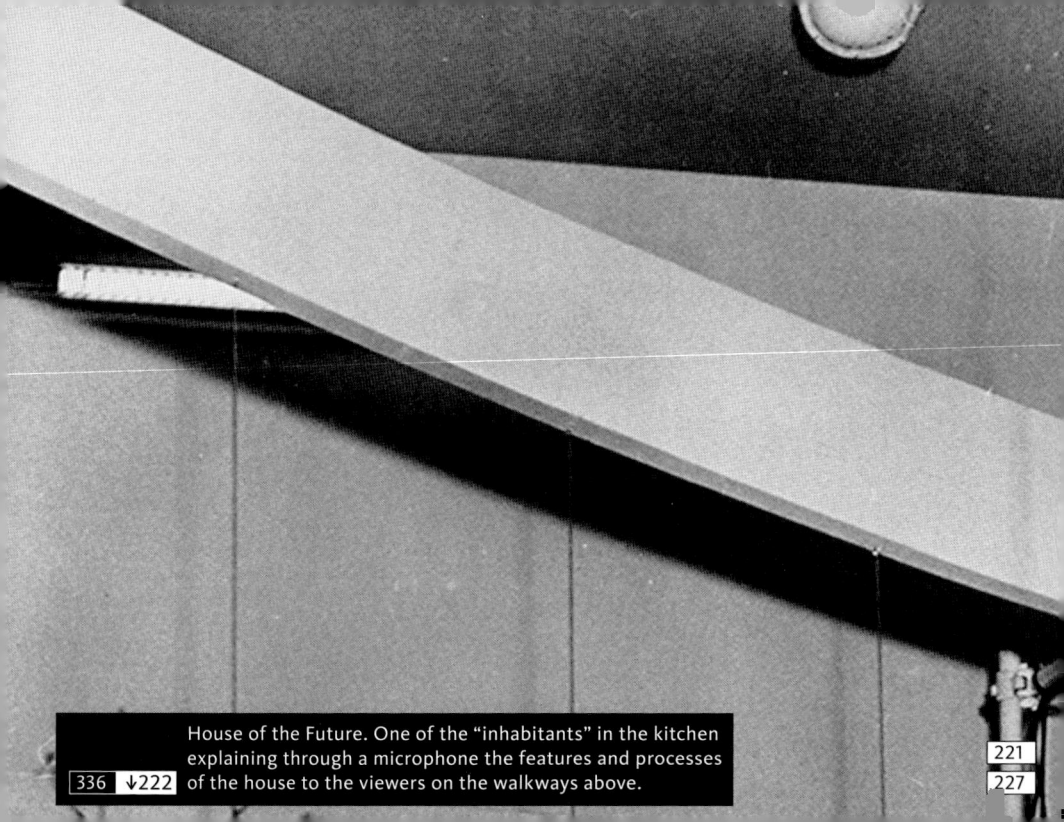

House of the Future. One of the "inhabitants" in the kitchen explaining through a microphone the features and processes of the house to the viewers on the walkways above.

House of the Future. View over washbasin onto patio with rainwater holder.
Photo: Associated Newspapers.

Caves Les Baux in Provence, France, 1953. Page from travel scrapbook.
Photos: Peter Smithson.

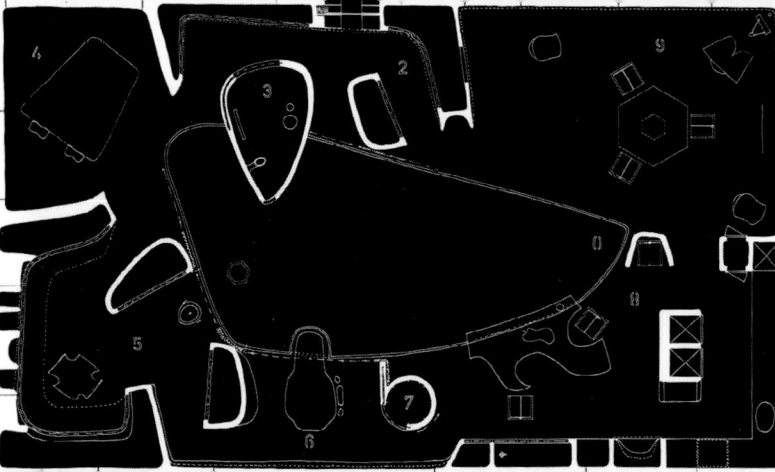

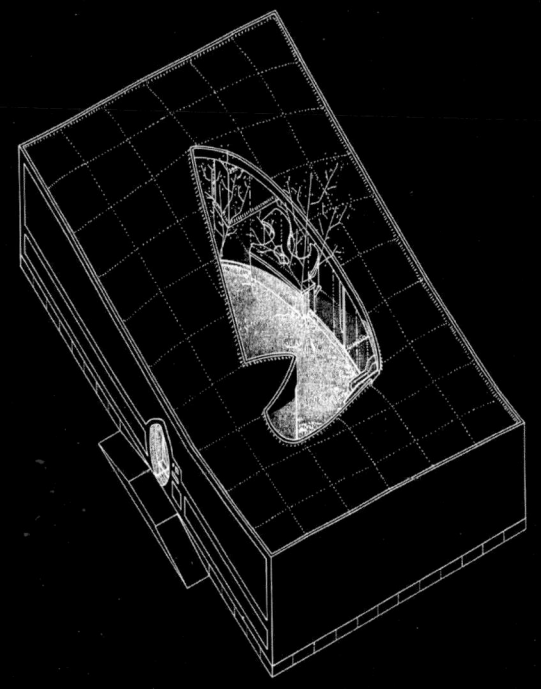

341 Volumetric drawing of the House of the Future, 1997.

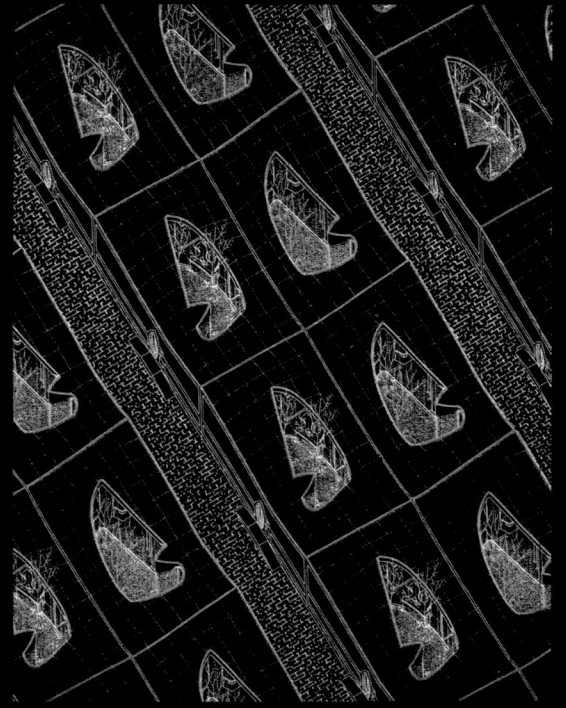

342 Volumetric drawing of mat cluster of Houses of the Future, 1997.

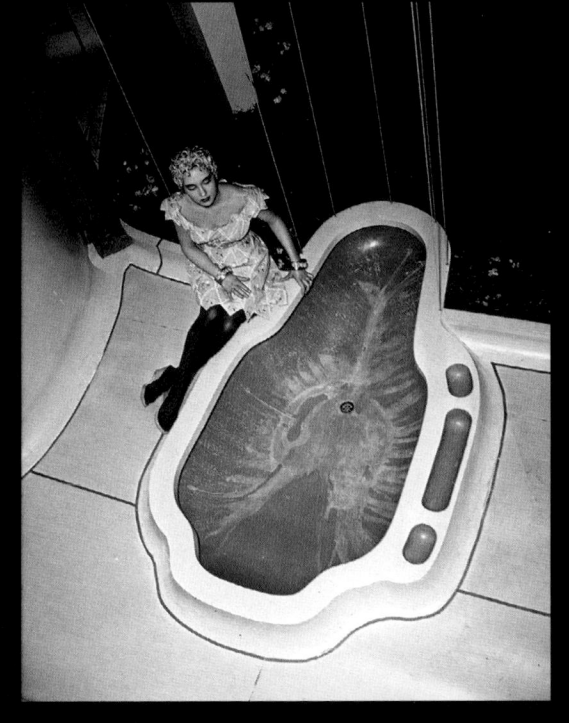

343 "Inhabitant" operating the self-cleaning bathtub of the House of the Future.

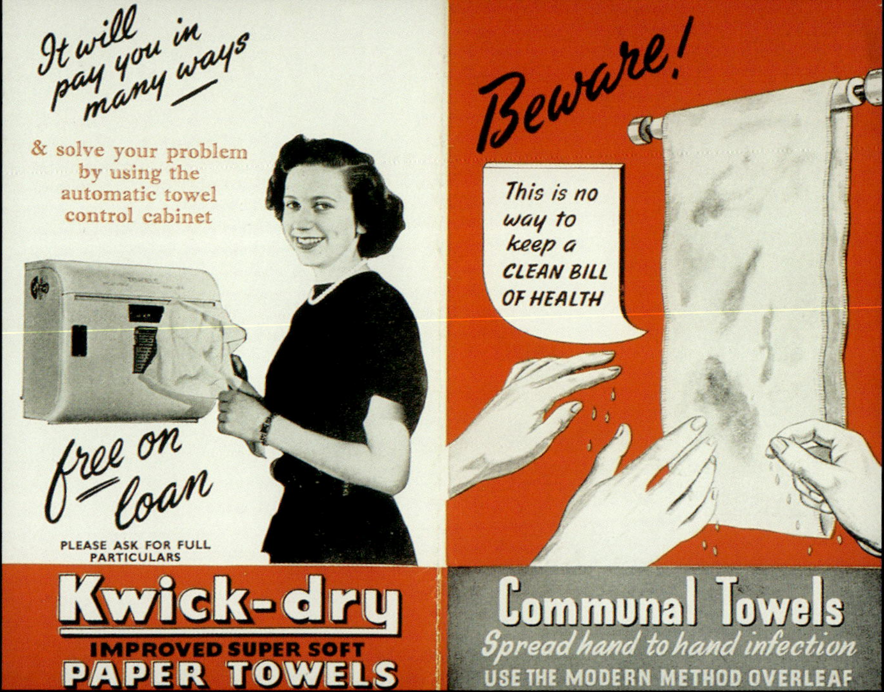

Advertisement for Kwick-dry paper towels. From the Smithson Archive.

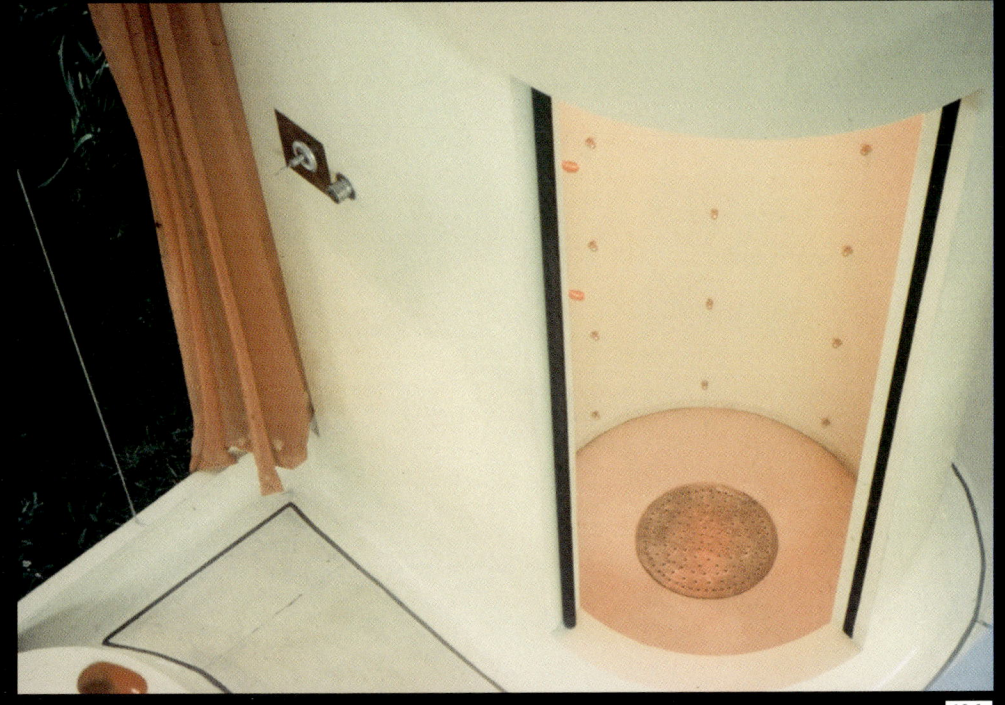

345 House of the Future. Shower.

346 R. Buckminster Fuller with a model of the Dymaxion House, 1927.

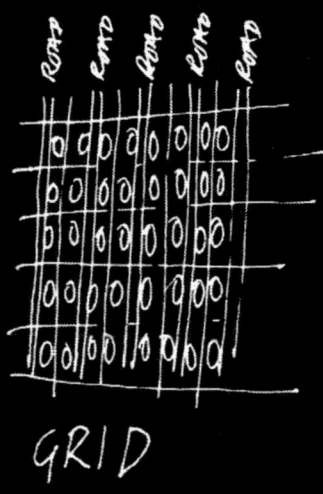

Alison and Peter Smithson, "Vertical Tube of Unbreathed Private Air," 1956. Diagram of House of the Future.

House of the Future, 1956. View from the patio into the kitchen.
Photo: John McCann.

349 Master of the Middle Rhine, *The Garden of Paradise*, ca. 1400.

Images of New York.
From the *New York Times*.

Martha Rosler, *Untitled* (O'Hare, 1989).
Courtesy of the artist.

353　Control room of EDS-NET (Electronic Data Systems Network).

Christopher Faust, *Suburban Documentation Project*.
Metro Traffic Control, Minneapolis, Minnesota, 1993.
Courtesy of the artist.

NASA Mission Control room during Apollo 11 Launch.

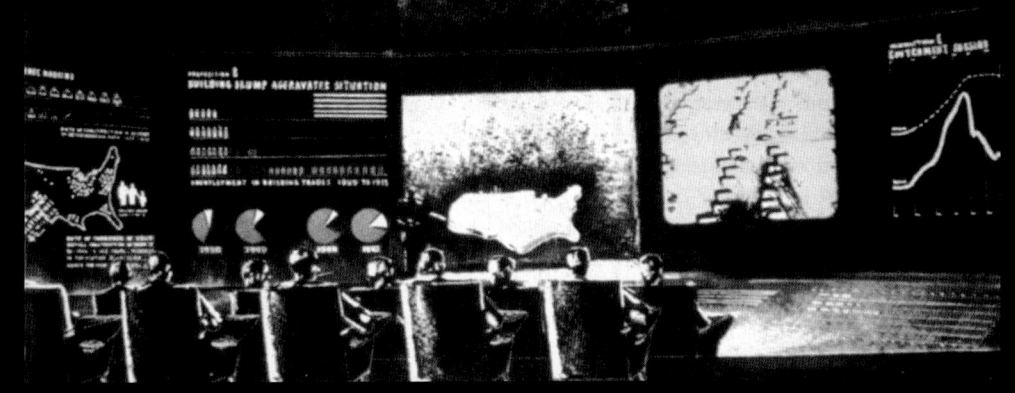

357 Henry Dreyfus, Presidential War Situation Room. Project view.

358 | Henry Dreyfus, War Situation Room as realized.

The American Exhibition in Moscow, 1959.
Photo: National Archives.

360 The Kitchen Debate in *Life* magazine.

Richard Nixon opening the American Exhibition in Moscow, 1959.
Photo: National Archives.

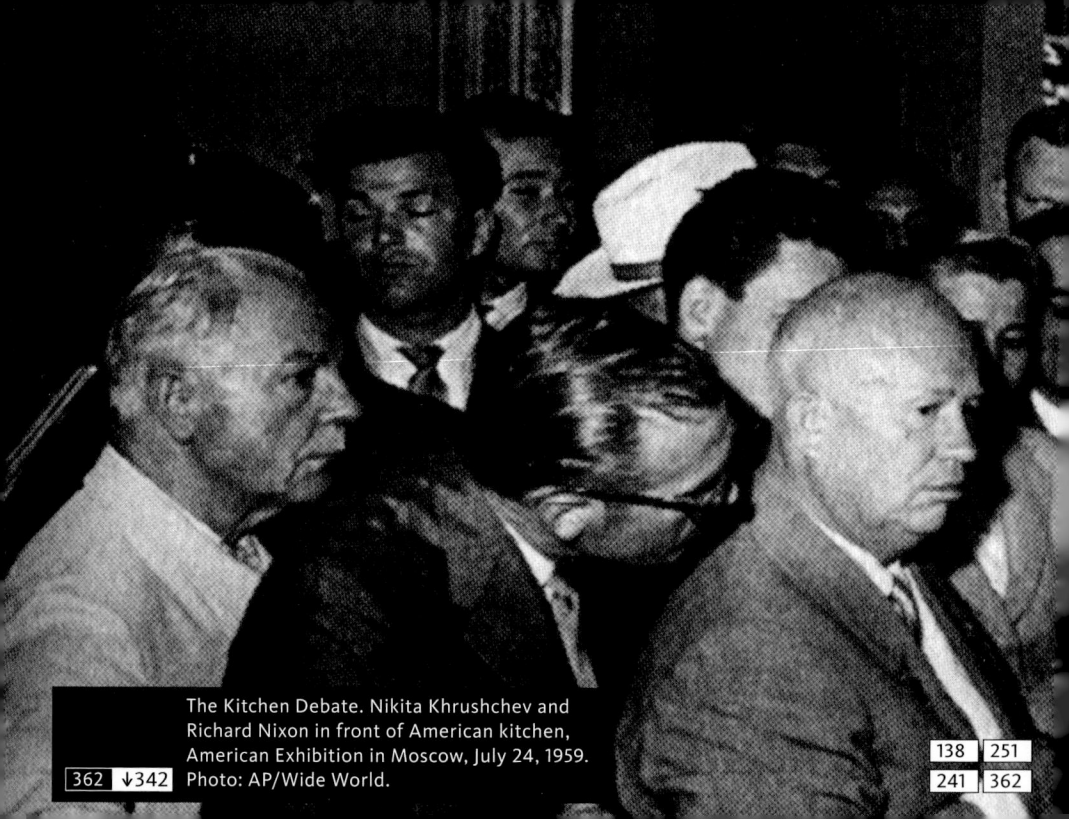

The Kitchen Debate. Nikita Khrushchev and Richard Nixon in front of American kitchen, American Exhibition in Moscow, July 24, 1959. Photo: AP/Wide World.

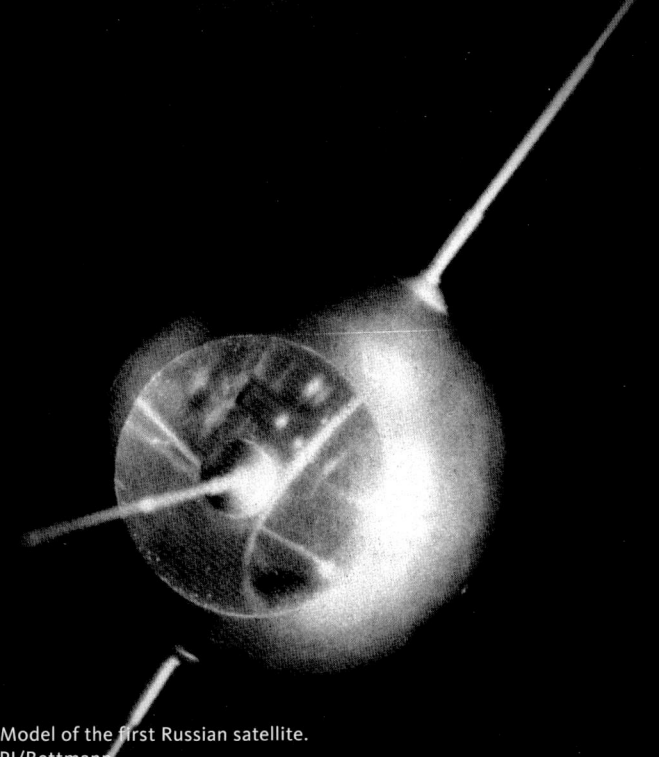

Sputnik. Model of the first Russian satellite.
Photo: UPI/Bettmann.

366 Advertisement for Hotpoint kitchens, 1950s.

367 Publicity photograph for Zenith "Strathosphere."

Buckminster Fuller's dome in the American Exhibition in Moscow. From *Life*, August 10, 1959.

American Exhibition in Moscow.
From the National Archives.

American Exhibition in Moscow. From the National Archives.

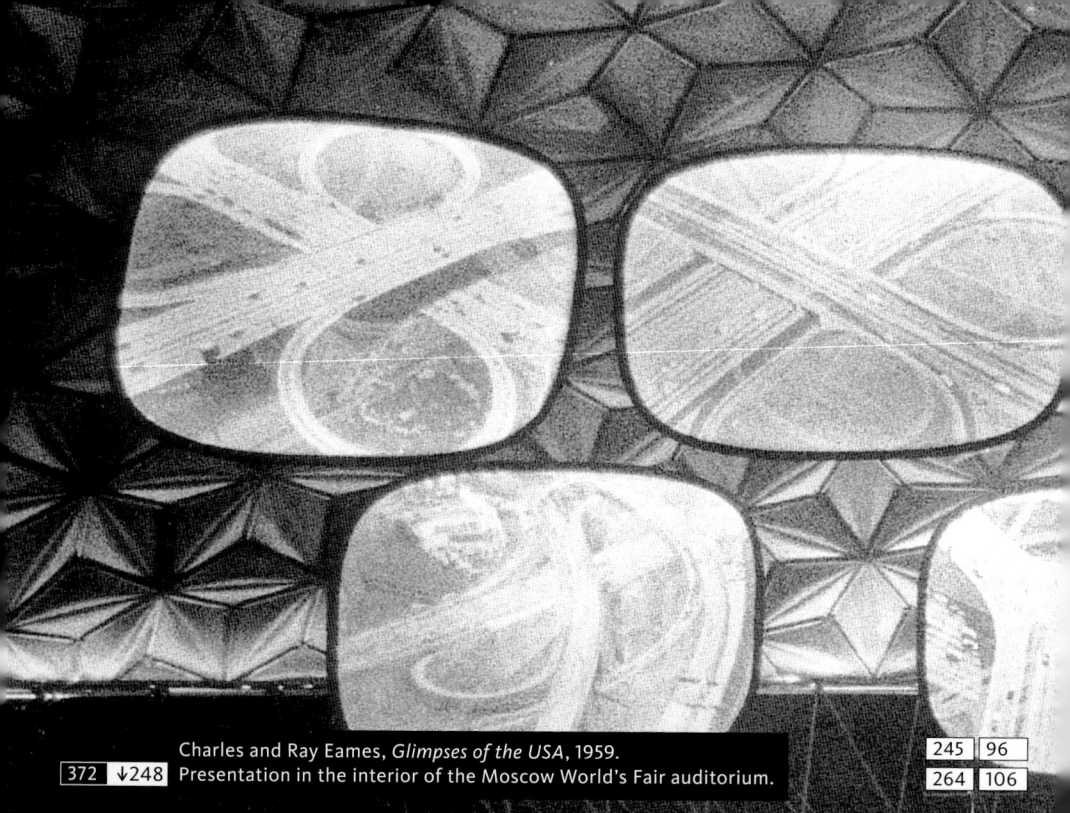

Charles and Ray Eames, *Glimpses of the USA*, 1959.
Presentation in the interior of the Moscow World's Fair auditorium.

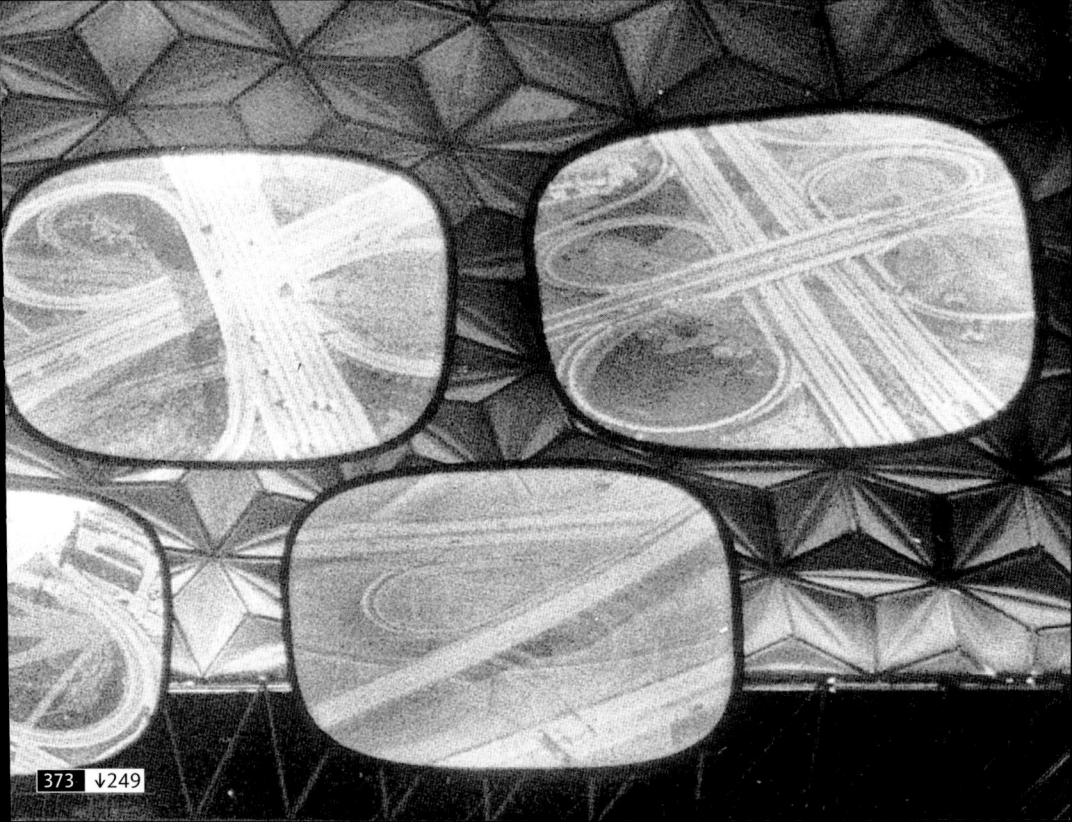

374 Charles and Ray Eames arriving in Moscow.

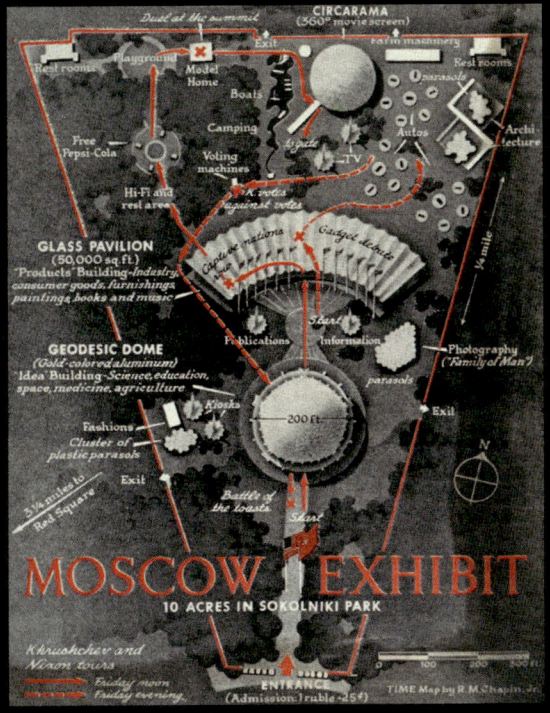

American Exhibition in Moscow, 1959. Plan.
From *Time*.

American Exhibition in Moscow, 1959. "Jungle Gym" structure filled with American consumer products, by George Nelson.

American Exhibition in Moscow, 1959. "Jungle Gym" structure by George Nelson inside the Glass Pavilion designed by Welton Becket. From *Life*, August 10, 1959.

Earlier version of Whirpool Miracle kitchen bound for a Milan trade fair. Courtesy Whirlpool Corporation.

RCA Whirlpool Miracle Kitchen at Moscow, 1959. The "Mechanical Maid" scrubbed the floor. Courtesy Whirlpool Corporation.

The Robotic Kitchen operated by a computer. Courtesy Whirlpool Corporation.

382 Charles and Ray Eames, sequence of frames from the film *Glimpses of the USA*, 1959.

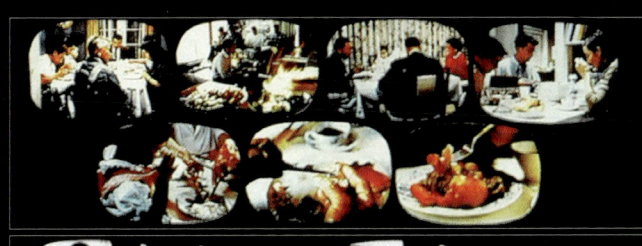
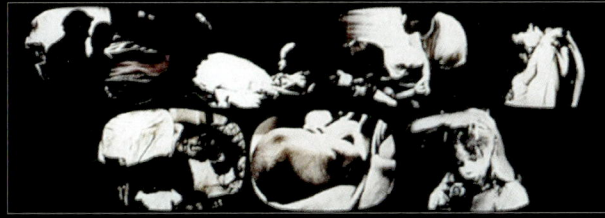

Charles and Ray Eames, *Glimpses of the USA*, 1959.
Presentation in the interior of the Moscow World's Fair auditorium, 1959.

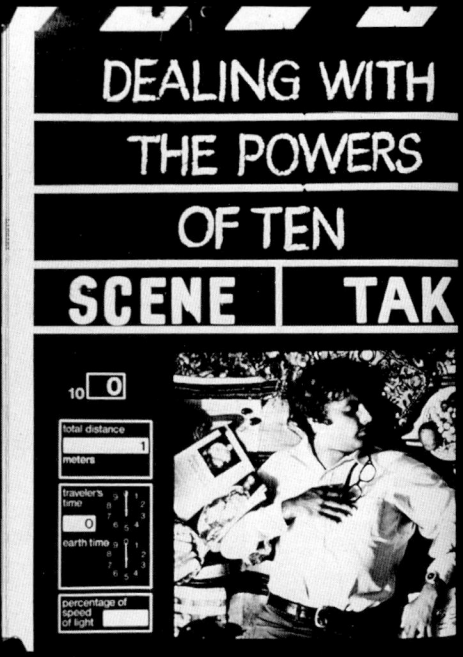

Charles and Ray Eames, *Powers of Ten*, 1968. A sequence of frames showing the progressive moves made by the imaginary traveler into space and back.

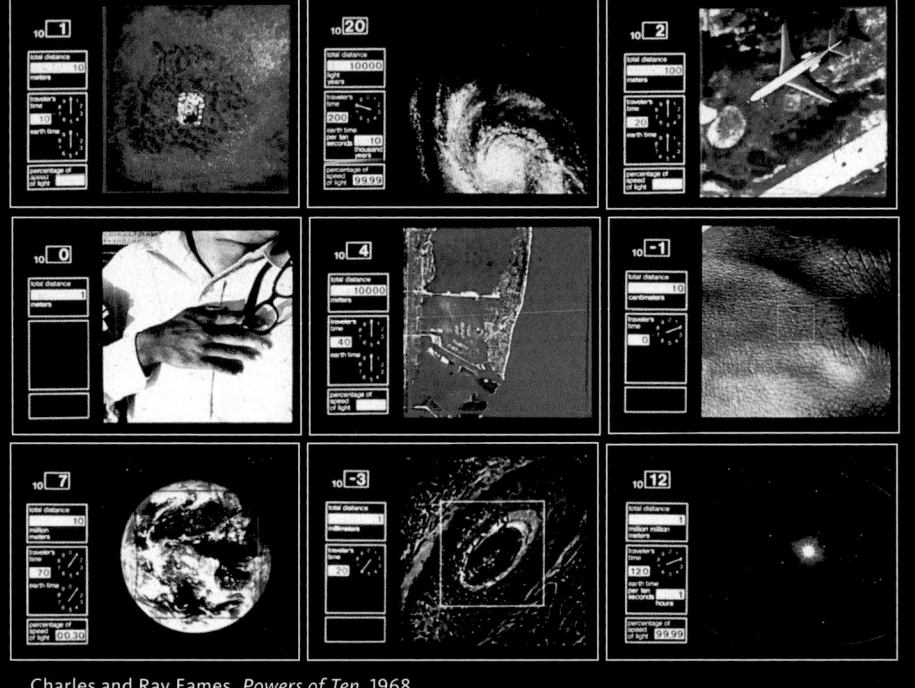

Charles and Ray Eames, *Powers of Ten*, 1968.
A sequence of frames showing the progressive moves made by the imaginary traveler into space and back.

Charles (in lift) and Ray Eames, outside their office filming the picnic scene for the first version of *Powers of Ten*, 1968.

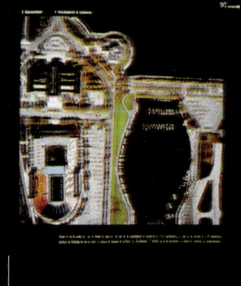
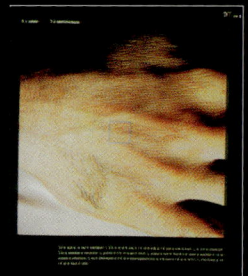

388 | Stills from *Powers of Ten*.

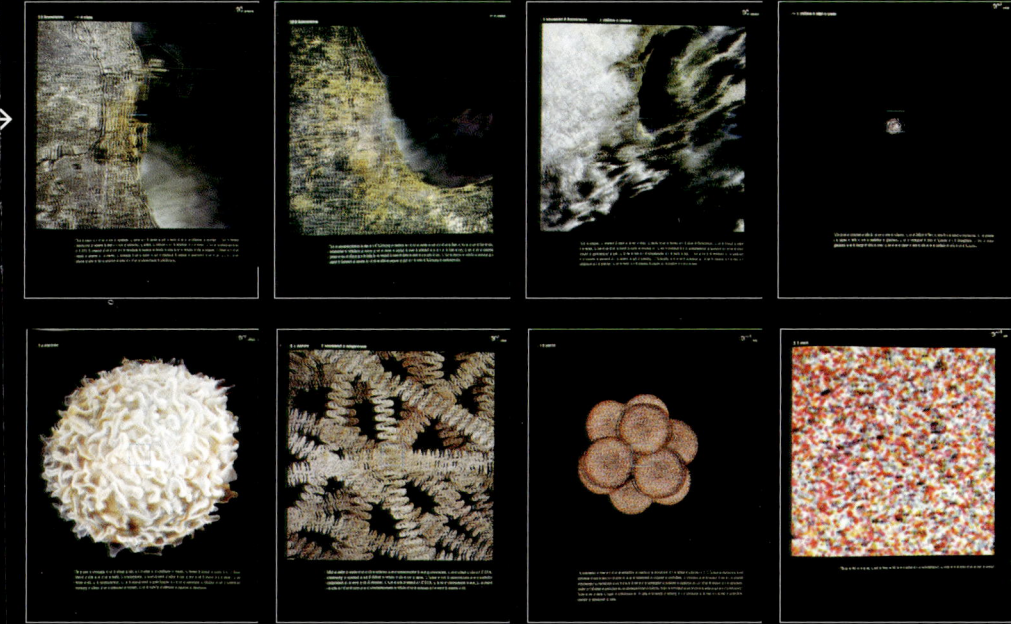

View of lecture hall at the second presentation of "Sample Lesson," University of California, Los Angeles, May 1953.

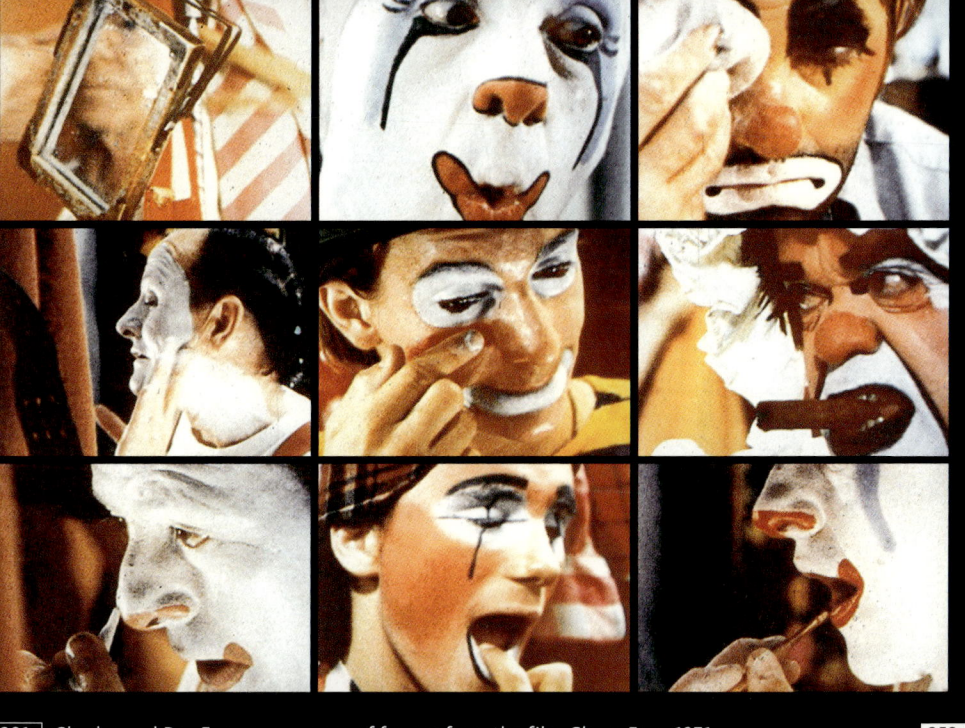

391　Charles and Ray Eames, sequence of frames from the film *Clown Face*, 1971.

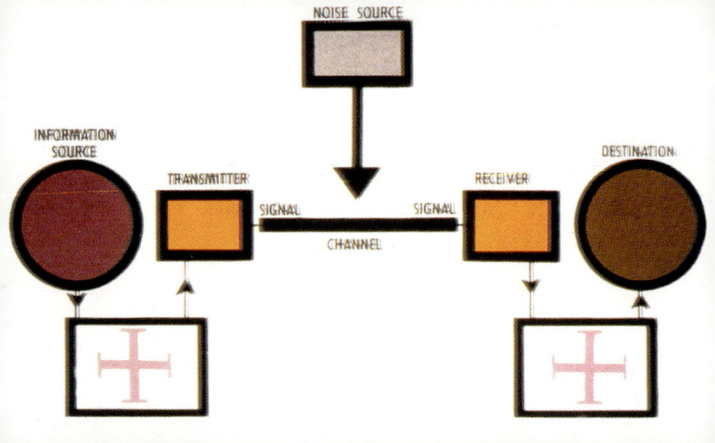

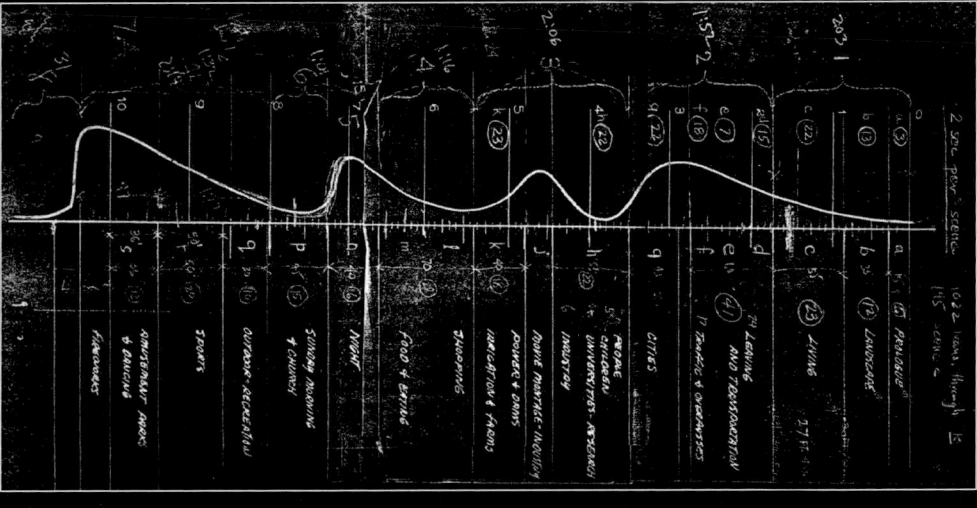

Charles and Ray Eames, notation of timing of sequences for *Glimpses of the USA*, 1959.
From Eames archives in the Library of Congress, Manuscript Division.

394 IBM Pavilion for the New York World's Fair, 1964–65. Exterior of Ovoid Theater.

IBM Pavilion for the New York World's Fair, 1964–65.
395 Under the Ovoid Theatre with host on the platform.

People Wall ascending into the Ovoid Theater at the IBM Pavilion, 1964–65. Photo: Gert Berliner.

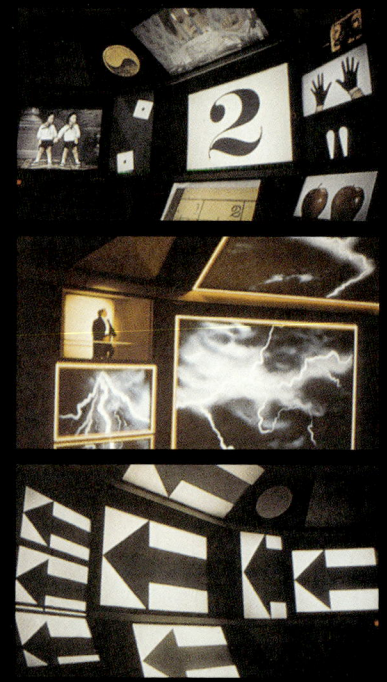

Details from the Eameses' film *Think*, a fourteen-screen presentation projected in the IBM Ovoid Theater. From *Industrial Design*, May 1964.

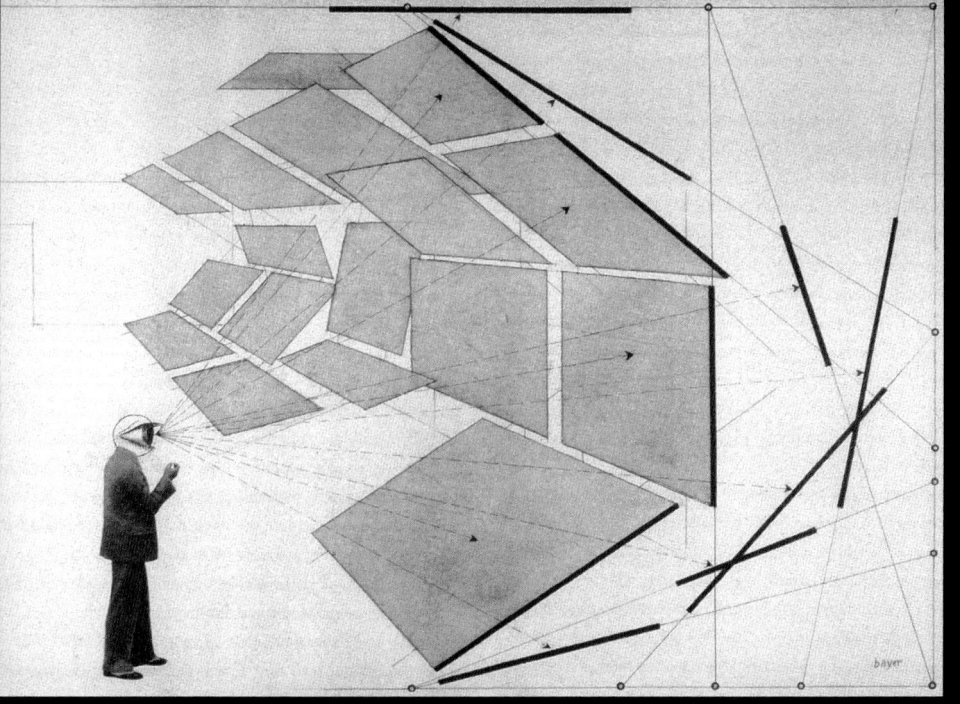

399 Herbert Bayer, *Diagram of the Field of Vision*, 1930.

IBM RAMAC 305 Computer (Random-Access Memory Accounting Machine).
Courtesy The Computer History Museum.

Big Board lists 4,000 questions about the U.S. that could be answered by IBM's RAMAC 305 computer. From *Life*, August 10, 1959.

402 Eames House, 1949.

403 Eames House, 1949.

405 Charles and Ray Eames, storage Units. Color sketch by Ray Eames.

Charles and Ray Eames, A Computer Perspective, 1971.
Exhibition view with visitors looking at History Wall.

Details of Eames House and studio from 1949 to 1978. Photos: Charles Eames.

Cover of *Life*, May 1, 1964, with the Unisphere,

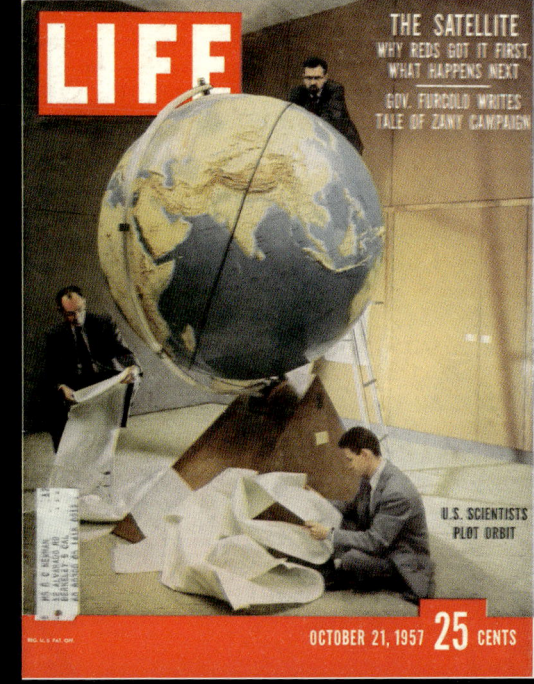

409 Cover of *Life*, October 21, 1957.

Pattern of orbits traced by the Sputnik in a typical twenty-four-hour period. From *Life*, October 21, 1957.

Aerial view of the World's Fair showing the US Rubber Ferris Wheel designed by Shreve, Lamb & Harman Associates. In the background is the Chrysler Pavilion.
Photo: Bob Golby, collection of the Queens Museum.

Environment showing Antarctic meteorology station located beneath polar ice.
General Motors Futurama pavilion, 1964 New York World's Fair.
Courtesy General Motors.

IBM's Computers at Work display designed by Charles and Ray Eames. Computers demonstrated how data written in Russian was easily and quickly translated into English.

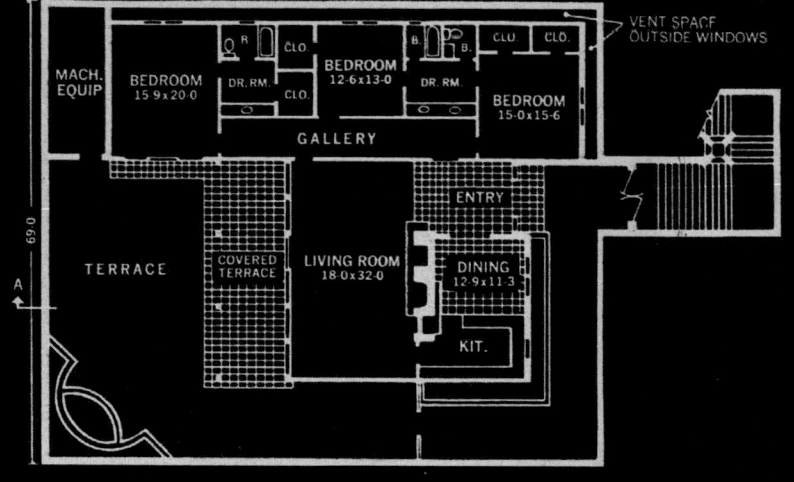

414 Underground Home pavilion in the 1964 New York World's Fair. Plan.

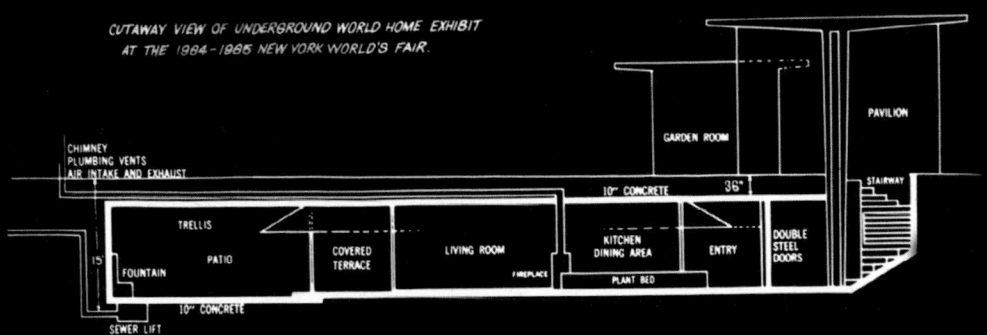

Underground Home. Section.
415 From *The Underground Home*, publicity brochure from the 1964–65 New York World's Fair.

Underground Home. Entrance.
Photo: Peter Warner.

Underground Home. Bedroom.
Photo: Peter Warner.

Demolition of the Underground Home pavilion. Photo: Bruce Davidson/Magnum Photos.

General Electric Pavilion, 1964–65 New York World's Fair. Courtesy Queens Museum.

Nuclear-fusion display in the General Electric pavilion.
Photograph courtesy of General Electric.

Thermonuclear Reaction at the General Electric Pavilion.
From *Life*, May 1, 1964.

"Underground Gardening": "Ninety-nine percent of the world loves nature—flowers, trees, green grass, hills, valleys and streams. Ninety-eight percent of us hate to take care of it, particularly in an *uncontrolled* situation where weeds and insects can invade flowers, and drought, wind or hail can destroy hours of labor—in moments. In an underground garden we deal with nature in our own terms." Courtesy Geobuilding Systems, Inc.

IBM Pavilion, designed by Eero Saarinen.
Photo: Bob Golby, Queens Museum collection.

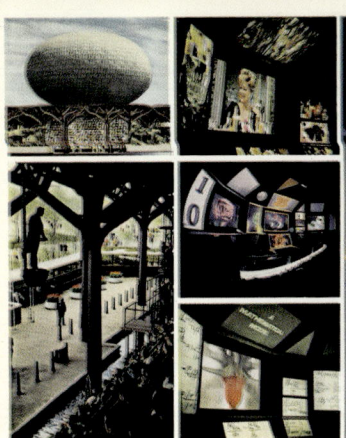

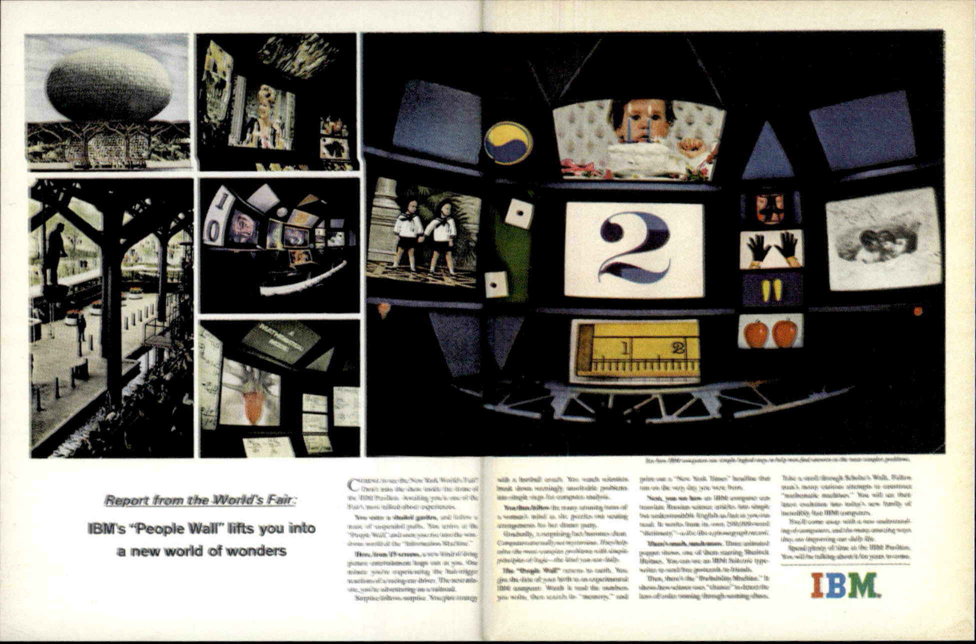
Report from the World's Fair:
IBM's "People Wall" lifts you into a new world of wonders
IBM

425 Magazine spread on the IBM Pavilion. 265

From *Life*, July 3, 1964. 284

Lunar Landscape roof of the Eastman Kodak Pavilion designed by Kahn & Jacobs. Photo courtesy of Photofest.

Futurama, General Motors Pavilion, 1939–40
New York World's Fair, designed by Albert Kahn.
Courtesy General Motors.

Spectators viewing the General Motors Futurama model at the 1939–40 New York World's Fair. Norman Bel Geddes Collection. Photo: Margaret Bourke-White.

Visitors to Futurama pavilion in sound-equipped chairs that travel around a 35,000-square-foot model on a simulated trip to 1960, 1939–40 New York World's Fair. Courtesy General Motors.

The Metropolis of 1960, Futurama pavilion, 1939–40 New York World's Fair. Courtesy General Motors.

Underwater motel, General Motors Futurama pavilion, 1964–65 New York World's Fair. Courtesy General Motors.

Underwater motel.
From *Life*, May 1, 1964.

"Road of Tomorrow," Ford Motor Company Pavilion, 1939–40 New York World's fair. View of the roof. Courtesy Henry Ford Museum and Greenfield Village Research Center.

Automated Superfarm in the desert, General Motors Futurama pavilion, 1964–65 New York World's Fair. From *Life*, May 1, 1964.

Martha Rosler, *Cleaning the Drapes*.
From *Bringing the War Home: House Beautiful*, 1967-72. Courtesy of the artist.

Martha Rosler, *Vacation Getaway*.
From *Bringing the War Home: House Beautiful*, 1967-72. Courtesy of the artist.

Len Jenshel, *Sterret, Texas 1985*.
Courtesy of the artist.

441 Living room in an underground house.

Andy Warhol, *Thirteen Most Wanted Men*, silk screen on canvas, 20 x 20 ft. Installed on the exterior of the New York State Pavilion at the 1964–65 New York World's Fair. Made of enlarged "mug shots" of criminals, the controversial mural was shown for a few days and subsequently removed. Photo: UPI/Bettmann Newsphotos.
Courtesy the Estate and Foundation of Andy Warhol, 1989/ARS New York.

New York State Pavilion at the 1964–65 New York World's Fair with Andy Warhol mural covered in black cloth. The mural had been whitewashed but could still be seen.
Photo: Peter M. Warner.

U.S. Vows to Destroy Iraqi Launchers While Israel Puts Off Any Retaliation

"Saudis Heed Call to Prayer in a Bomb Shelter."
From the *New York Times*, January 19, 1991.

Kosuke Tsumara, *Final Home Jacket*, 1995. From MoMA, *Spring 2006 Catalog*.

"Gas Masks: Survival in the 90's!" Advertisement.
From the *New York Times*.

Photo: Mikael Olsson

Beatriz Colomina is Professor of Architecture, Director of the Ph.D. program in Architecture and Founding Director of the Program in Media and Modernity at Princeton University. She is the author of *Privacy and Publicity: Modern Architecture as Mass Media* (MIT Press, 1994) and *Doble exposición: Arquitectura a través del arte* (Akal, 2006), the editor of *Architectureproduction* (Princeton Architectural Press, 1988), *Sexuality and Space* (PAP, 1992), and coeditor of *Cold War Hot Houses: Inventing Postwar Culture from Cockpit to Playboy* (PAP, 2004).